M4
SIGHTS
GUIDE

Mike Jackson

Severnpix

Design: Lisa Griffiths

ACKNOWLEDGMENTS

Our thanks to all the people who told us what went on where they lived or worked, and to the librarians who swiftly directed us to relevant local history references.

Thanks to Gil Jackson for logistics, indexing and chauffeuring; to Jonathan Holder for evaluating legal matters, and to John Elkington for managing our website.

For railway history consultancy and contemporary accountancy, we are as always in debt to Chris Burnley.

We are extremely grateful to Ian Davies and his colleagues at the Museum of Welsh Life for kindly providing us with Welsh road sign translations, pronunciations and meanings, as presented on Page 87.

THE M4 SIGHTS GUIDE

ISBN 0-9545402-2-0

First published by:
Severnpix
P.O. Box 468, Worcester WR6 5ZR
16th July 2005
www.severnpix.co.uk

DISCLAIMER

INTRODUCTION

What sort of book gets a review in The New Statesman, Practical Caravan, the Lancaster Guardian and Auto Express?

It could only be the M6 SIGHTS GUIDE, published in November 2004.

Joe Moran in the New Statesman said "It was a tough job but someone had to do it – travelling up and down Britain's busiest inter-urban motorway writing thumbnail sketches about the landmarks that can be seen from it."

Well, I didn't have to do it. I chose to do so - for four reasons: one, it is genuinely fascinating to find out about things alongside the carriageways (Put that man down as an anorak!); two, you give pleasure to a number of residents or workers who occupy premises adjacent to the road: from being the sufferer of a nearby thoroughfare, they become an informed commentator whose views are sought, valued, and recorded; three, unquestionably the Guides enrich people's journeys, giving them some information and insights about what they are passing; and four, given judicious research, logistics, design, printing and distribution, you can make a small profit on the endeavour.

Moran reckons motorway tourism might seem a bizarre pastime. Well, I agree. I never intended to encourage people to make a journey specifically to allow them to evaluate dozens of structures for five seconds at least and thus be enlightened by our entries. I very much hope no-one has been daft enough to do that. But if you need to travel from A to B via a major motorway, then, with one of our Guides, you hopefully have a better experience whilst heading along that relentless corridor of tarmac.

When you do examine every edifice that you pass on such a journey you inevitably assemble a slice of life, capturing aspects of urban sprawl, farming practice, work patterns, depot deployment. Go from one end to the other of the book, and hopefully you have sharpened your appreciation of a number of institutions, issues, businesses and phenomena that were previously just a fuzz in some other part of the country compared with the bits you know reasonably well.

THE M6 SIGHTS GUIDE was the cheapest Auto Express Christmas 2004 stocking filler recommendation: "A fascinating collection of entertaining trivia to make the miles fly by."

The Lancaster Guardian considered the book was meticulously researched. This view wasn't shared by the London Guardian's David Ward, who demonstrated that he knew parts of the hinterland better than me, and decided the publication was "less a travel guide than a compendium of everything trivial, bizarre and even ludicrous."

A journalist from the Lichfield Mercury was furious that we had not included his beloved cathedral in our reference to the city. He was missing the point. Everyone knows about that wonderful building, and every sheet of tourist literature drools over it. We try to avoid replicating the obvious and so focused on something about which most M6 users would be unaware.

Since the emergence of our M6 book, two orbital motorways have been tackled by other writers: 'M25 Travelling Clockwise' by Roy Phippen is a charming presentation of Iain Sinclair's "collar" (see our Page 74), and, framing Manchester, 'Around the M60', went down well with David Ward. Maybe it was the coffee table form that appealed, as the M60 tome weighed in at £24.95, compared with our mere £9.99.

We admit to being arbitrary and brief, and what Ward thought eccentric, we like to think of as a sense of humour. We believe people want to be cheered up on their arduous journeys, and to be able to recall a joke at times when they pass a particular point.

That was the reason we made up our Knutsford entry – but immediately declared our deceit right there on the page. We didn't visit the place nor examine any historical literature. Instead we put in a joke. (This is what comes of having written hundreds of scripts for 'Call My Bluff'. You start to think that only one in every three things you say needs to be true.)

We supplied review copies of our book to many of the regional newspapers, but didn't bother with the ones based in towns where we'd said something rude. Hence the Knutsford Guardian didn't receive the Guide in the post, but they heard about it on local radio, so e-mailed us for more information, wanting to know: "Is the journey past Knutsford interesting? What features are described in the Knutsford part of the book?" And: "How did you investigate the sights around Knutsford?" We salute their forthright journalism. I phoned them to break the news that the Knutsford entry might not be their cup of tea and, to their immense credit, they gave us a very good review a few weeks later, once they had seen the book, and the joke.

There are no made up bits in this book. We have researched every entry. It may have resulted in trivia, but what do you want? The Encyclopaedia M4ica?

We have limited space and finance.

At one stage I feared there was no Sight Guide in the M4. There are those long stretches either side of Newbury where the road seems to lie in a ditch surrounded by foliage, fencing or anonymous fields.

It was using the route with colleagues from the BBC in Bristol, who despaired of the dullness of the much-repeated journey, that made me determined to overcome such shortcomings in sights. Even if there was nothing to photograph, I decided to find out something about the corridor through which the carriageway passes, to improve the travel experience of regular users

Newcomers to our Sights Guides should to take a little time to comprehend how the layout works. In essence, we force the carriageway into a straight line, in this case running left to right – representing west to east – and assume it occupies an endlessly elastic world wherein we can squeeze and stretch various objects around the motorway until they neatly occupy the space available above and below our representation of the road.

Our Guide must work in both directions, but inevitably the layout of our pages, with the west at the front, will tend the reader to approach London from the provinces, ultimately from a different country.

I had some sense of occupying different territory either side of the Severn estuary, but what impacted on me more strongly was a sense of traversing the economic scale as one moved eastward. If we crudely consider our journey as taking us from the Welsh valleys and dropping us in west London, we pass through a complete spectrum of societal circumstances.

At one end of the M4 are the grandchildren of coal miners and steel workers, living far better lives than their forefathers, but nevertheless sometimes in frugal, limited communities. Two hundred miles down the same road we are a stone's throw from Kensington, Chelsea, Belgravia.

You can't help but notice the difference between the shoppers on the Kings Road and those in Merthyr Tydfil. There are distinctions in manner, wardrobe, physicality. The Welsh will hail each other, strike up conversations with friends and strangers, displaying an appetite to pass the time of day with a fellow citizen, whereas in and around Harrods we can witness postures of purposeful confidence as the well-heeled march arrogantly from coffee bar to clothes rail, avoiding eye contact whilst snootily evaluating the fashions of their fellows.

We travel through pockets of under-privilege and over-privilege. A 'reliable domestic cleaner' in rural Berkshire commands £7 an hour to hoover the halls of the landed gentry, whereas you can get a room at the County Hotel in Ebbw for just £13 a night.

We encountered the electioneering of May 2005 whilst sensing the texture of materialism across the whole spectrum of British society. We deduced an alarmingly simple yardstick to determine the political colour of a constituency: the density of swanky vehicles. Once someone's got a BMW, they are lost to Labour; yet the party displayed no plans to reign in the excesses of disposable income. They discreetly shore up the base of the pyramid, but dare not tamper with the top.

There can be a chilly air round parts of Berkshire; grim-faced toffs terrified that lesser mortals might impinge on their good fortunes. From our dips into a cross-section of communities we would report that money ain't necessarily buying happiness.

Yet material wealth is the driving force of much of our society, and life along the M4 reflects the machinery and application of that agenda. We are relentlessly plundering the planet to indulge our every whim, and it's not obviously making us better, or more cheerful.

The book is a great leveller. The curious juxtaposition of entries which the format of our pages throws up will amuse you. And as well as a heap of facts, we believe we have captured something of the contemporary character of a slice of our nation's life.

I found the journey fascinating and fun, and I hope that you will be enriched by some of the information and observations contained within these pages.

OUR FRIENDS FROM LONGBRIDGE

As readers of our M6 SIGHTS GUIDE will know, MG Rover very kindly saw fit to support our research undertakings by lending us a fine 45 Club SE with which to travel that corridor. (They had seen how we had run up 140,000 miles in our old Rover 214, which is still going strong!)

We were delighted to be able to travel in style and pleased to place some panels promoting MG Rover cars to our readers.

Come January 2005, we announced we would tackle the M4 and again MG Rover kindly said they would be happy to operate a similar arrangement, and invited us to choose the most suitable car for the purpose, with a view to us buying it from them upon the completion of the task.

We went for another 45 Club SE, this time a four-door 1,400cc model (kinder to the environment), and started our researches.

Like many, we were terribly saddened to learn of the events at Longbridge through the Spring of 2005.

We see no reason not to proceed with including panels advertising the fine MG Rover cars once again. There are hundreds of loyal dealers around the country who have vehicles on their forecourts and are keen to sell and then service them.

The new Rover 45. Refinement within reach.

Quality comes as standard with the new Rover 45. With distinctive good looks, impressive performance and handling, coupled with a superbly comfortable ride, the restyled saloon and five-door hatchback models are a very attractive and highly accessible proposition.

This pioneer of practicality will deliver you to your destination with the minimum of fuss, but with the kind of civilised elegance you'd only expect to find in a much larger car. All this, plus an unrivalled choice of high-spec equipment and greater passenger and luggage space than many of its more expensive rivals.

You can pay a vast amount of money for a car that's this good. Or you can buy a new Rover 45.

A CLASS OF ITS OWN

IMPORTANT NOTICE TO DRIVERS AND READERS

Drivers must not use this book whilst travelling. Additionally we recommend that passengers do not read the contents aloud whilst the vehicle is moving. Please devote 100% concentration to safely driving along the motorway.

Drivers must take sole responsibility for driving safely on the motorway and elsewhere. To the fullest extent permitted by law the authors and the publisher exclude their liability for loss or damage arising from any misuse of this publication.

Beth yw ystyr y gair yna?

That's Welsh for: What does that mean?

We don't think we were alone in driving along the M4 in Wales and thinking Abertawe was a different place from Swansea.

For newcomers to the Welsh language we have provided a listing of the translations that appear on road signs west of the Severn. It's on Page 87.

WELCOME ABOARD

You're travelling to London, which, if you don't stop for fuel (or a rest) you can reach in three hours. (It took us 6 months!). Your driver today will concentrate on the road ahead, but passengers may care to enjoy the scenery, and in particular the 500 things we've chosen to draw your attention to over the 79 pages ahead. To fully understand how this book works, please take time to study the Principles and Practice page at the back. Please note, the Department of Transport recommend a 15 minute break every two hours.

AFON GWIL

This meanders southward passing twice under the M4, first from east to west under Junction 49, then a mile further south, back west to east. But we straighten out the M4 to run left-right so the river goes underneath our version from above to below, then, further along, from below to above. Don't worry, you'll get the hang of it.

Carmarthenshire

We generally avoid replicating what you can find in tourist literature, but when you're here we do recommend you track down, and then climb up to, the most elaborate dining facility ever constructed, William Paxton's banqueting tower on top of a hill at Llanarthne. Celeb spotters may want to hang round Laugharne in the hope of sighting hotel owner Neil (We buy it all at Do It All) Morrissey.

Pontarddulais

We stayed at the Fountain Inn on the A48. It's where the Daughters of Rebecca rioters plotted their destruction of the Bolgoes Toll-gate in 1843. The restaurant is full of wonderful old photos and some artefacts from the local colliery. The Llwchhwr Star we picked up headlined the funeral of a man killed in an accident at the local steel works.

Ammonford

John Cole of Velvet Underground used to play the church organ here.

Oakwood

Pembrokeshire's answer to Alton Towers, boasting a Vertigo extreme flight experience, Disco Inferno and Dixie's Chicken Diner.

PONTARDDULAIS-LLANELLI

A single track commuter service from Shrewsbury. In 1911 Llanelli rail workers were killed by Worcester troops during the first national Rail Strike.

J49   5187   J48

PONT ABRAHAM SERVICES

Staffer Jim Connolly told us he finds lots of lost property here, not least mobile phones and even car keys. One night a drunken woman roared in and over-turned her car by the petrol pumps, simply grazing her nose in the process. Abraham was a farm worker who used to prop up the bridge.

GEIBREN FARM (E.O.)

Selwyn Anthony looks after these 80 acres that are home to 40 breeding ewes and 8 horses. He can't persuade his son to come back from Canada and take the place over, and his daughter Judith is not interested in farming. She works for the Reading Evening Post. Doubtless she'll want to study this Guide before she next heads over to see Mum and Dad.

LOUGHOR BRIDGE

The Loughor is joined by the Ammon south of Ammonford and later forms the estuary south of Llanelli, north of the Gower.

National Botanical Gardens

Opened by Prince Charles on 21st July 2000. We liked the Alfred Russel Wallace garden, dedicated to the Welshman who came up with the concept of the origin of the species but was pipped to the publicity post by Darwin. Digestible panels explain the DNA of an onion. We suggested they ask BP to sponsor a hot house.

Carmarthen

200 years ago this was a far more important place than Cardiff, but it never became a conduit for coal and so stayed in the doldrums, which of course may not entirely have been a bad thing.

St Clears

It's not clear why St Clears gets a sign along here, because you can only get to it by passing Carmarthen and the only thing important about St Clear is that it's where you veer south-west off the A48 on to the A477 if you're taking a trip to Tenby. So a sign for the colourful seaside town might have made more sense.

LLANDEILO TAL Y BONT

There's not much left of this little Llandeilo. The best part was carted off to St Fagan's last year – the old St. Teilo's church, being lovingly re-constructed at the Museum of Welsh Life. This old house, that was next door to the 13th century church, is being restored as a private home. Meanwhile the church will be restored to its condition of 1520.

Llandeilo

This is the proper Llandeilo, (15 miles north, on the A483), which has a main street almost devoid of chain stores, but with a big Co-op lurking on its fringes. We liked the relaxed atmosphere of the CK supermarket and the stuff in the 'The Last Century' antiques shop, where we bought an old guide book to the Chilterns.

City and County of Swansea

More or less the whole of the M4 in Wales used to lie within the enormous, powerful county of Glamorgan, that covered a triangle between the Gower, Merthyr and Cardiff, but local government re-organisation changed all that, so now between here and Newport (that was in Gwent) we have a series of smallish counties, each dominated by one urban area, this, the first, heading east.

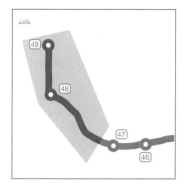

GORSGOED FARM

Stephen Jones cheerfully fattens up 300 head of beef cattle here, across 100 acres split by the motorway. He prefers to deal with local butchers rather than the supermarkets which frequently change their requirements and buying prices.

Llanelli

Some times you have to take a stand on things. And if you are 15 burly and talented rugby players, then why should you be pushed around. We don't much understand rugby, but we understand that Llanelli are a pretty strong side with sponsorship and benefactors, unlike the boys over at Swansea. The Welsh Rugby Union proposed a sort of merger of the Llanelli and Swansea sides, that hasn't gone down at all well here. You could say they've kicked it into touch.

Pembrey Country Park

Where were you go for skiing and tobogganing? Not to the seaside, surely. Oh, yes you would. Artificial Alpine activities are amongst the attractions of this massively reclaimed stretch of coastline beyond Llanelli that used to house an armaments factory. Dogs are not allowed in the Adventure Playground, and Nudity is not permitted on the beach.

PENDRE FARM (W.O.)

This is a good place to explain something of our modus operandi (how we do stuff). We scour the sides of the carriageway for sights, then use an Ordnance Survey map to find the place. We knock on the door and ask questions. If there's no answer (as was the case here) we leave a leaflet and a note on our letterhead, asking the occupiers to get in touch. We included a stamped address envelope here, but they didn't respond.

BAGLAN-MILFORD HAVEN

You build a line from London to Bristol, and from Gloucester to Milford Haven, seven foot gauge all the way. Some achievement, but Brunel's followers never liked his gauge. They couldn't wait to change it to our standard 4 feet 8 and a half inches.

Gorseinon

Keith Morgan's study charts the rise and fall of some fundamental industries in these parts: Mountain Colliery opened 1846, closed 1921. Monach vitriol works: 1869 - 1921. Grovesend Tinplate Works: 1886 - 1953. Gorseinon steel works: 1890 - 1957. Mardy tinplate works: 1910 - 1957. Bryngwyn steel works: 1897 - 1951. Bryngwyn sheet metal works: 1908-2001.

Felindre

At this hillside hamlet we had an excellent supper in the Shepherds Arms which was built and run by David Harris (1848-1938), one of the founders of the Miners Federation, after he retired from Pentrefelin Colliery. You can see most of the Swansea coastline from the hills.

WHERE ARE THE WELSH PLACE NAMES?

For reasons of space we've devoted Page 87 to translations, pronunciations and explanations.

AFON LLIW

Managing water round here can be quite a problem. Fresh water reaches Swansea from the two huge Lliw reservoirs north of here. Meanwhile the Environment Agency Wales issues a special guide for older people about being prepared for Flooding: "Plan your escape route, particularly if you live in a bungalow."

SWANSEA WEST SERVICES

After our brief visit to the Angel Inn at Kenfig (page 20) and a starlit view of the sparkling steel works at night, we eventually found our way here at 10.30 in the evening. Good news was that the Travelodge had a room available. Bad news was it didn't have a bar, which by this time we would have appreciated. Good news was the site has a Little Chef with Beer and Wines on the menu. Bad news was "Licensing Laws prevent the sale of alcohol at motorway services." Excellent Valleyways tourist display panels in the car park, including "The hard harvest of the valleys." Next door is Penllergaer Forestry Commission woodland.

SUSPECT

We walked down a bridle path with our Ordnance Survey map open and were accosted by a lady who thought we were trying to steal cow manure from the field behind her cottage. She'd seen a jogger hop over her gate and had put grease along the top of it so next time he'd fall flat on his face.

SPEED CHECK

Driving along country lanes near here we came across a couple of guys from Solargen installing one of those solar powered speed readers to alert you to your speed as you enter a built up area. The firm's UK operation is based in Cwmbran. They install safety street furniture all over the country. Solar panel driven machines are ideal where there is no mains power supply nearby. The solar power charges a battery which in turn powers the device. Even on a cloudy day the panel will gather enough energy to sustain the unit for several days.

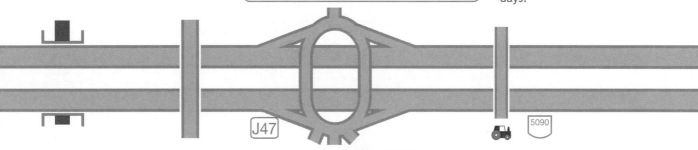

J47 5090

3M (E.O.)

How about this for a water tower. Over 400 people work here making disposable nappies, coated adhesive tapes and specialist aerosols like Spraymount. It's 3M's biggest plant outside the US, and was a key centre for video tape production.
What are the three Ms? Minnesota Mining and Manufacturing. They started off a century ago doing sandpaper, then moved to sticky tape, but made biggest impact with Post-it notes. Hope that'll stick.

Swansea

We found a fascinating two shilling Glamorgan County Handbook dating from the 1950s (Inside is an ad for the new Ford Prefect at £395 plus purchase tax of £165.14.2). A. Willis Pile of the Swansea Chamber of Commerce noted: "Swansea has all the amenities which could have made it an ideal holiday centre. A number of light factories have been set up which it is hoped will offer employment. It must be stressed that light industry cannot possibly take the place of heavy industries and it is on the latter that the prosperity of the port and town must depend. The town is destined to become one of the most modern and splendid in the West."
Two of the town's most influential characters were not Welsh: Walter Pockett, master mariner and shipping entrepreneur, who established Pockett's Wharf came from Gloucestershire, and James Abernethy, who designed most of the docks, came from Aberdeen.
You need to see some of the aerial photographs of the docks to appreciate their scale and complexity in their heyday. Find them in the Maritime Museum that is being embraced by the new Waterfront Centre. Get a copy of the marvellous Stony Stories portfolio and explore the whole stylish harbourside area. Smart buildings, boats, and promenade; great statues and other works of art; a sort of sexy, cheerful confidence about the place.

AFON TINPLATE

Most of this plant is hidden by trees, but as it's pursuing a very old local industry, we thought you'd want to know about it. They supply plain, printed and coated tinplate in sheet, strip and body-blank form, turning out 35,000 tonnes a year. They've got an automated four-colour print line with ultra-violet curing. So, who would want stuff like that? Perhaps Envases, down the road at Port Talbot, who make aerosols.

SWANSEA NORTH SUB STATION

This is a National Grid base transforming the overhead line from Pembroke to Merthyr Tydfil. The conductors carry 400 kilovolts. In the Spring of 2005 Eve transmission were in the midst of replacing insulators, fittings and earth wires on the towers, and even working their way by harness along some of the conducting cables.

VARIABLE MESSAGE SIGN

The first of many heading east, this one normally promotes Swansea Park and Ride services. Just £1.50 a day for the car and a free ride for everyone inside into town and back. But you must return by 7 pm.

J46

Llangyfelach

This is one of the oldest parishes in Wales, having been founded by St David back in the sixth century. The largest agricultural fair in Wales used to take place here around St David's Day. Rowan Williams, the current Archbishop of Canterbury, went to school not far from here. These days the place is host to a daily ad hoc Park and Ride operation that is mostly set around the front of the Plough and Harrow.

Dan-yr-Ogof Caves

Most people who have gone underground in this part of the world were forced to do so to earn a living. So why did a couple of farmers climb into a hole? Because they were the intrepid Morgan brothers, always game for a challenge? Or maybe they were hoping to find coal below their land? Anyway, they squeezed into a big cavern and 90 years later there are 100 giant fibreglass prehistoric monsters across the fields above, and it's called the National Showcaves Centre for Wales.

LLANGYFELACH TOWER (E.O.)

This was part of the parish church until a severe storm two hundred years ago meant the main building had to be  demolished. It sits in the grounds of the new church which was awash with helpers when we visited, dusting and hoovering with determination prior to the arrival of the Bishop of Swansea that Sunday for confirmations. The ladies drew our attention to the painting of Holy Communion at Pentonville Prison by local boy Evan Walters, who was inside only as an artist in residence.

DVLA HQ

An absurdly large structure in the middle of a housing estate on a hill. It looks like it's escaped from a Manhattan side street. Built in the 1970s, it's home to 5,000 workers for the Driver and Vehicle Licensing Agency, who receive 80,000 items of correspondence and 50,000 phone calls every day. It's not true they can read your tax disc with binoculars from any north facing office window.

YNYSTAWE CRICKET CLUB

They just had a tatty wooden hut as their club house, but then they successfully applied for a lottery grant and got this nice new building, which they share with the Football Club who play round the back. The cricketers won the British village club championship, thrashing Derbyshire's Elvaston at Lords no less. The side are sponsored by Executive Travel, who ferry people along the M4 and are looking forward to our Guide.

RIVER TAWE

On the blue destination signs next to the name Swansea, we see Abertawe, which means the mouth of the Tawe. It was always an important natural harbour, and, when this area became the centre of British copper production, artifical additions were added.

Down at the dock side these days the emphasis is understandably on tourism, but the port remains an important trading conduit handling timber, glass, liquid bulks and steel; and you can get a ferry to Cork.

Pontardawe

There was once 16 miles of Swansea Canal dug along the west side of the Tawe as far as Abercraf, but most of it's been filled in. However you can explore a stretch that runs through this town where Neath Port Talbot Council base their Enquiry Office.

CLYDACH-BAGLAN

The bridge carried a mineral line off the Neath-Milford Haven track, but it's now closed.

Neath Port Talbot County Borough

Their Civic Centre is based in Aberafon. The receptionist lives in Llanelli and travels 20 miles a day to get to work. Their Tourist Information Centre is at the far end of the Vale of Neath in the village of Pontneddfechan. Kill for a copy of their Top 10 walks fold-out map. It's superb.

NEATH-SWANSEA

In the Spring of 2005 three transport operators were in competition to win the seven-year franchise to run the Great Western service between Paddington and Swansea: Stagecoach, National Express and First. Stagecoach run South West Trains and claim this would be a logical extension, National Express run Wessex Trains and Swansea-London coach services. First reckoned they should continue doing a great job.

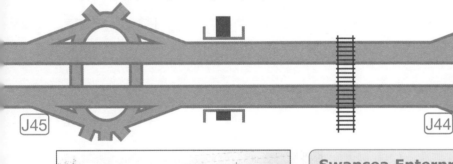

J45 J44

TAWE RAILWAY BRIDGE

Westward the Milford Haven-Neath line disappears into the mile-long Llangyfelach tunnel. The Welsh are big on railway tunnels: under the Rhondda mountain was a nearly two-mile standard gauge, now closed, and up at Blaenau Festiniog is a narrow gauge job at over two miles. The tunnel under the Severn estuary is a stonker, but, of course, only half of that is in Wales.

Swansea Enterprise Park

Sounds like the city's answer to silicon valley, but in fact it's just a big, mixed bag industrial estate, occupied by the likes of PC World, huge gas tanks, blokes fixing old lorries and, not least, the West Wales animal and pet supplies warehouse. Most enterprising thing was giving it such a fancy name.

To be fair, it was the UK's first experimental Enterprise Zone of 1981, and the council planted loads of trees and stuck in a lake.

EBENEZER CHAPEL, LLWYNBRNWYDRAU

The Foundation Stone was laid by the Rev. Edward Matthews of Bonvilston in the 50th year of his ministry, Oct 6th 1881. Some of the most elaborate memorials (all inscribed in Welsh) we have ever seen in the locked-up graveyard.

National Waterfront Museum

We are immensely excited about this place which will patently answer all the questions we struggled to deal with in getting a sense of the scale, circumstances, social implications and mechanics of Welsh industry and enterprise. It's a comprehensive centre documenting and celebrating the history and capacity of industrial endeavour across the country. Corus are even providing a Rolling Mill, so we can understand something of that vital activity. It's due to open in October as part of the Trafalgar celebrations (Swansea tinplate sheathed Royal Navy ships).

Briton Ferry

Great artefacts at the Library, founded by the Countess of Jersey in 1901: a huge Victorian mooring buoy from the Brunel Dock discovered in 2 metres of silt during M4 viaduct excavations; a Roll of Honour to the 100 employees of the Villiers Tinplate Company who joined HM Forces for the "European War 1914-19" (of whom 11 fell in battle): and testimonies for Captain Routledge's Emigrant's Life Belt, "ready for sea in under one minute, can be used by a Lady as well as a Gentleman, contains a spirit flask, biscuit tin, signal flag, foghorn, whistle, souwester hat and large knife." Down the road, excellent cod and chips for £2.90 from the Moby Fish Bar on a Sunday night and great bread and cakes from the Jersey Bakery on Monday morning.

LOCAL LINKS

The Welsh Assembly deploys two co-ordinators in each of four Welsh regions to talk through policy with locals, who can also monitor what's going on in Cardiff by visiting www.webcasting.wales.gov.uk.

RHONDDA-SWANSEA

As soon as coal mining and iron puddling got serious in the valleys, canal and rail routes down to the coast became vital. There were two options from Merthyr Tydfil, one directly south through the Taff Valley to Cardiff, the other westward through the Rhondda Valley, then the Neath towards Swansea Bay. Here we pass over two tracks that were part of the western road/canal/rail options, one either side of the Tennant Canal.

Merthyr was a vigorous crucible for the demands for workers' rights. Passionate rallies over the 1831 Reform Bill led to the slaughter of dozens by a detachment of the Argyll and Sutherland Highlanders. The radicalism did not die however and the people of Merthyr tenaciously pursued the working class struggle. We recommend you read Gwyn Williams's 'The Merthyr Rising'. See our bibliography on page 95.

TENNANT CANAL

Opened for business in 1824, this links Aberdulais with Port Tennant in Swansea. It lies to the west of the River Neath, whilst the Neath Canal, which stops just short of the M4 at Briton Ferry, runs along the east bank of the river, joining the Tennant at Tonna.

You can join the Canal Preservation Society's regular work parties, safeguarding and promoting the waterways.

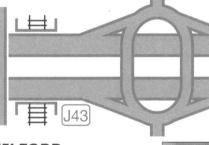

J43

MILFORD HAVEN/BRITON FERRY-BITUMEN TERMINAL

A key freight artery that brings bitumen from the Coryton Refinery in Essex to the BP Bitumen terminal, a blending plant which produces the Olexobit range of binders used in a variety of applications including thin surfacing asphalt, porous asphalt and stone mastic asphalt. Yes, the stuff that makes up the surface of many of our roads. The properties of the materials have a reputation for not cracking at low temperatures and not deforming at high temperatures. They also have good adhesion, cohesive strength and fatigue life, which, let's face it, is what you want from your roads.

HOLIDAY INN EXPRESS

Yes, it's another of those instant landmarks. This one opened in 2003 with 70 bedrooms, and is doing so well, it was having another 20 rooms (currently going at £79.95 a night) added in the Spring of 2005.

GLAMORGAN HEALTH AND RACQUET CLUB (W.O.)

"Congratulations! You've taken the first step towards a fitter and healthier you." Options include: Pump Overload, Power House Moves and Ashtanga. But you must obey Studio Etiquette: Please arrive on time to avoid injury and prevent disruption.

Gower

Doing the furniture round for the Llanelli Antiques Roadshow, we heard a charming lady at the end of the peninsula say two things we'd never heard before: "We bought this place from the National Trust" and "I didn't like my husband's helicopter, so he got rid of it." She had lots of fabulous furniture but it was too far for our van to reach, so she came to the show by car with some wooden Welsh spoons.

The Heritage Centre was commended by the British Guild of Travel Writers as Best Tourist project of 1995. "We don't make it easy to join the Guild. There are several hoops to jump through." Readers will not be surprised to learn that we're not members.

BRITON FERRY STEEL WORKS

Beyond the A48 viaduct, down by the east bank of the Neath, we can see what was once an important plant. Serious injuries were inevitably common amongst steel workers, but here one of the bosses was a victim. In January 1893 company director Isaiah Bevan walked under a crane whilst it was unloading materials when the chain broke, causing the load to drop on him. He died the next day.

GIANT'S WHARF

The Briton Ferry Stevedoring Company is based here, loading ships with scrap metal for Spain, new plate iron for Ghent and new coils of steel for northern Spain. They receive loads of reinforcing bar from Turkey and Spain, and bulk animal feed and house coal. It takes about 2 days to load or unload, and movements in and out of the sea are tide dependent.

A 48 VIADUCT

This big bridge well downstream of Neath provided a welcome relief for that town when it was constructed in 1950. Snaps of the work in progress in the Angel Inn at Kenfig (Page 20).

OUR LADY OF THE ASSUMPTION

The fancy bell tower was standard issue from the Cardiff diocese architect when this place was built in 1965. The bell is rung every Sunday and at funerals.

J42

FLO-GAS DEPOT

You wouldn't want to light a match round here because the place is full of pipes and cylinders containing combustible materials. Flo-Gas distribute household and vehicle LPG (liquid petroleum gas) from this site, which they share with Transco.

WELL SPENT

The Welsh Assembly is not without its critics, but casting a glance over its endeavours and procedures in this part of the world indicated to us that it declares its intentions, then commits its resources to make measurable improvements to the regional facilities and fabric. There is a healthy documentation of spending goals. Meanwhile farmers moaned to us about being bumped up Council tax bands, and the Port Talbot Guardian condemned local boy Sir Anthony Hopkins for not spending more of his fortune in town.

RIVER NEATH

This runs in a remarkably straight line for most of its 12 mile length down the Neath Valley, before twisting south to flow into the north east corner of Swansea Bay.

Throughout the 19th century the mouth of the river was bustling with shipping, shipbuilding and ferry services. Brunel brought his wisdom to bear on the creation of a floating dock which allowed for the regular handling of bigger vessels. It opened in 1861 and by the end of the century was exporting 120,000 tons of coal a year.

LIGHT POINT

This piece of sculpture has been designed by John Gingell to mark the rejuvenation of the area. It's the second tower on the site. The first was designed by Brunel to house an innovative hydraulic lift mechanism that was a key feature of the Briton Ferry floating dock. Our picture shows the whole of the structure, though from the elevated motorway you can only see the top of it. The Baglan Energy Park designers had wanted the tower to be a lot taller, but the Highways Agency reckoned it would be distracting. Next year there'll be a big Italian tissue paper mill behind here.

Vale of Neath

GWR issued a South Wales Travel Guide in 1907, which told readers that the "Great Western Railway has, as it were, brought the Vale of Neath to the very gates of Swansea. A visit to Neath may be regarded as one of the indispensable features of a tour through South Wales. It would be difficult to imagine a more delightful spot for a summer holiday than this fairy-like tract of sylvan scenery."

Neath

We spent a night in the Castle Hotel, previously occupied by Lord Nelson, Lady Hamilton, Richard Burton, Elizabeth Taylor, Harry Secombe and Neil Kinnock, all of whom would have enjoyed a quiet night, which was not our experience as it's now sadly at the heart of the local binge-drinking-in-and-out-of-noisy-bar circuit. The inaugural meeting of the Welsh Rugby Union was held here in 1881. And they've got the steps that Nelson used to launch himself into the four-poster.

PINE TREE CARS

"No deposit needed. Refused Credit, we can help you. Our deals are fantastic, you can pay by plastic. Any old car as your deposit regardless of its age or condition. Five hundred vehicles on the forecourt at any one time."

£500 REWARD

At the other end of what is now the M4, at Windsor Castle, just 150 years ago, Queen Victoria and her Privy Councillors issued a Proclamation: "Whereas in certain districts of south Wales tumultuous assemblages of people disguised and armed with guns and other offensive weapons, have taken place by night, and outrages of the most violent description have been committed upon the lives and properties of divers of our subjects, and whereas in contempt of the restraints of law and order, these tumultuous assemblages have pulled down toll-gates, and have violently entered and destroyed toll-houses and whereas they have also attacked the mansions of individuals, extorting from them sums of money by threats or by violence, and have destroyed by fire the hay, corn and other property of diverse of our subjects. We have thought fit to command all Justices of Peace, Sheriffs, Under Sheriffs and all other Civil Officers that they do their utmost to repress all tumults. As an inducement to discover offenders we do hereby promise and declare that any persons who discover and apprehend perpetrators shall be entitled to a Sum of Five Hundred Pounds. Victoria R."

TECHNIUM

This is a sort of incubator facility for new hi-tech firms developing commercial applications relating to fresh energy sources and environmental chemistry. Technium Sustainable Technologies is an initiative of the Welsh Assembly's department of Economic Development and Transport.

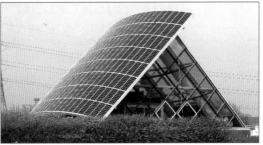

SOLAR CENTRE

How do you convince the G8 Summit of your environmental credentials? Knock one of these up and stick it outside the Conference Centre in Birmingham in 1998. That's what BP's Solar Division did, after which they brought it here and handed it over to the council to make it a Visitors Centre for the Energy Park. The 176 photovoltaic panels will generate 12 kilowatts on a good day.

BAGLAN ENERGY PARK

BP had a stonking big chemical works here until recently. Now it's a 21st century smart technology complex. Elsewhere, the world's second biggest oil producer has a way to go environmentally. They generated 85 million tonnes of greenhouse gases in 2004.

MANDERWOOD (W.O.)

They are one of the biggest and longest established manufacturers of roof trusses in Wales. They've been doing it here for 15 years, and supply the structures right across the country.

SCOTT (W.O.)

This is where the Andrew Scott construction company keep their kit. One of their biggest local undertakings in recent years was the re-building of furnace No5 at the Abbey steel works following a fatal accident there in December 2001.

GE POWER PLANT

A new £300 million station that utilises the H system, comprising a gas turbine, a steam turbine and a generator, able to produce 480 megawatts of electricity with a high level of efficiency and low level of emissions.

A GRAND OCCASION

It's hard to imagine the social structures of working communities a hundred years ago. For an insight into a highly-layered world, get hold of a copy of E. Humphries's 'Reminiscences of Briton Ferry and Baglan' of 1898, and now available as a reproduction in local libraries. "In 1888 the Victoria Works of the Villiers Tinplate Company were incorporated. The ceremony of starting the engine was gracefully performed by Miss Davey (Woodside) amidst great cheering, and in the presence of the principal commercial men of the district. The banquet subsequently took place in the new assorting room which was decorated with a profusion of exotic plants, kindly sent from Woodside, and neatly arranged by the head gardener (Mr. Lloyd), and a grand display of buntings and mottoes, such as "Long life and prosperity to the Directors and Managers".

The number that sat down to the banquet was about 250, and the event is regarded as one of the greatest which has ever occurred in this neighbourhood in connection with its industries. The brass band of the First Glamorgan Artillery Volunteers was present, by the kind permission of Major Gardner. The toast of "The Royal Family" was proposed by the Chairman. Mr M.G. Roberts proposed that of "The Bishop and Clergy". Mr D.T. Sims proposed the health of "Lord Jersey, Governor of New South Wales." Mr Hunter, chief agent of the Briton Ferry estate, referred to the great interest Lord Jersey took in Briton Ferry, assuring the audience that there would be no one more pleased to hear of that great gathering than His Excellency."

BAGLAN RAILWAY STATION

Arriva run an hourly service between Swansea and Port Talbot, but only every other train stops here. Not one vehicle in the car park at 10.30 on a Friday morning. Maybe people are arriving here, to walk over the motorway to work in the Energy Park? Meanwhile the Council is spending millions on improving the motorway junctions.

ST CATHERINE'S, BAGLAN

Mr and Mrs Griffith Llewellyn of Baglan Hall had this place built for £15,000 in 1882. He was buried here in 1888; Madelina Georgina joined him in 1903.

TALBOT GATEWAY

Old Baglanites can remember when there was a police station here. Now it's office space, as yet unlet, but capable of accommodating 500 call centre operatives or 200 office personnel (who need more space and a couple of cupboards – not just a chair, screen and ear-piece).

PANASONIC

You've probably got something in your car that was made here. Now, what could that be? Your speakers. Most cars manufactured in the UK acquire their speakers from this place, and there is also a considerable export market in their well-respected product. The plant opened in 1998 and employs 250 people. And guess how many sets of speakers they turn out in a year? Eight million!

ENVASES

A Spanish firm that do deodorants, or monobloc aluminium aerosols to you.

Aberavon

The year is 1922 and Aberafon needs a new Labour parliamentary candidate, whilst an ex-Leicester Labour MP needs a new seat. He had been deselected in the Midlands as a result of his pacifist stance in the First World War. So the Scot came to south Wales and wooed the local socialists. It was a happy marriage and Ramsay MacDonald became the town's MP and Labour's first Prime Minister. MacDonald had a vision, but it didn't include a dedicated personal jet ski section of the beach, which is what the town has these days.

YOU CALL THAT HARD WORK!

South Wales was a powerhouse of the Industrial Revolution, generating and manipulating the two fundamental ingredients of industrialisation, iron and coal, which determined the look of the landscape and the circumstances of the people.

Landowners discovered the potential of the wealth that lay below their fields, entrepreneurs devised means of accessing and utilising these minerals, workers became adept at toiling in difficult and dangerous circumstances, and transport companies commissioned engineers to establish effective means to traffic the raw materials and processed goods out of the valleys and down to the sea.

All this enterprise made a small number of resourceful individuals, who mostly had financial assets to begin with, immensely wealthy; and it provided fairly steady employment for many thousands of labourers. It also created a middle class – the works managers, who thanked God for their good fortune every Sunday in one or other of the many churches and chapels they set up.

Some communities occasionally behaved like the hierarchy was a natural order of things: mass flag-waving when the propertied patronised the poor with the provision of a parish hall for the welfare of the workers. But there was also a fuming vein of anger at the abuse, brutality and arbitrariness of prosperity in the midst of poverty that cultivated the trades union movement and eventually brought about the application of some universal rights and social facilities.

Local MP Dr. Hywel Francis takes a keen interest in current developments. He's chairman of the Westminster Parliamentary all-party steel group, and in May 2005 was re-elected to represent Aberavon with a 60% share of the votes cast.

RIVER AFON

This runs south-westerly from Glyncorrwg, through Cwmafan, to form the fresh(ish) water element of Port Talbot inner docks.

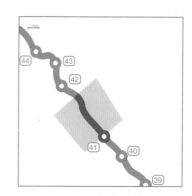

GORWELION

Designed in the 1970s by Cowbridge architect Keith Evans. Not, as rumour would have it, built by Richard Burton for his Mum.

J41

EXCEL

When you press a button on a vending machine, how does the thing know what to do? It all hinges on the wiring and triggering mechanisms some of which are manufactured here.

LOOKING FOR CREDIT?

"Join the money revolution," invited leaflets for the Credit Union being offered to people in the hospital lobby.

NEATH PORT TALBOT HOSPITAL

270 beds of which 28 are dedicated to patients with mental health problems. It was opened by Prince Charles in February 2003. We took our snap, then wandered in an open door at the rear of the building and found ourselves in the mortuary.

ST MARY'S, ABERAFON

This was built in 1857 to replace an earlier church that had been severely damaged by flooding in the previous century. Sally Roberts Jones's excellent 'History of Port Talbot' analyses an 1875 photograph that shows the tower, surrounded by thatched cottages, dominating the essentially rural town, with smoking chimneys of new tinplate works visible beyond.

ABERAFON HOUSE

Council offices for some education, social services and finance staff. In the library next door, a West Glamorgan Archive Service display of Ordnance Survey maps for 1884, 1900, 1921, 1948 and 1984 shows the dramatic development of Aberafon from a hamlet on the river bisected by a single railway line.

SARON CHAPEL

The original Methodist chapel of 1867 was re-built in 1914. It says 'Trefnyddion Calfinaidd' on the front which Ian Davies tells us means Calvinistic Methodists.
There's a footpath up to it, which is good because you dare not park outside - on a busy, narrow road on a bend.

Port Talbot

Some docks were constructed near the little Welsh town of Aberafon towards the end of the 19th century by the enterprising Mansel Talbot family. Then in 1894 the Port Talbot Railway and Docks Company started to exploit the growing prospects for exporting coal and iron. A community grew around the wharves and rail head, and it soon became known as Port Talbot - the place, as opposed to the maritime facility. After WW2, Margam Moors was chosen as the site for Britain's first integrated steel works, and so Port Talbot became a much more important town than Aberafon to its north.

TESCOLAND

Have you noticed the number of Tesco artics along here? They're keeping the shelves stacked on all the stores they have in south Wales. In some places it's not just Tesco in the town centre, Tesco is the town centre. Along our route the brand pervades Swansea, Neath, Port Talbot, Bridgend, Pontyclun, Pontypridd, Merthyr, Tredegar, Ebbw Vale, Barry, Penarth, Caerphilly, Cardiff, Newport, Pontypool and Chepstow. There's a Tesco car park tucked below the carriageway between Junction 40 and 41.

WILSON'S ROOFING

They specialise in Welsh slate and have fixed everything from garages to Margam Castle. They need the sign so people can find them.

HOLY CROSS

The St Theodore's Parish Council health and safety audit has identified and marked headstones in a potentially dangerous condition: "Do not touch or approach these monuments".

J40

CIVIL AND MARINE

What happens to all the slag that is a by-product of steel production? It goes into this new plant here where it's turned into Ground Granulated Blastfurnace Slag, GGBS, that can be added to concrete to improve durability in structures subject to aggressive environments. They produce half a million tonnes a year, some of which is sold across south Wales, the rest shipped abroad from their dedicated berth.

ABERAVON RUGBY FOOTBALL CLUB

We can see the lighting stands that service the stadium in which the Wizards hold their own in the Welsh Premier Division. They have been in existence since 1876 and have provided the Welsh national team with nearly fifty players over the years, who between them have gathered 227 international caps, biggest collection having gone to lock Allan Martin. The ground is completely boxed in by terrace houses that change hands from around £90,000.

STEEL WORKS

This is unquestionably the most impressive sight visible from any motorway in Britain. The Corus plant occupies a site 1 mile across and 2 miles long. We have identified the 10 biggest structures that our motoring machines made of metal (some of which may well have come from here) pass by.

POWER PLANT

This unit is dedicated to providing electricity and steam for Blast Furnaces 4 and 5. Waste gases from the blast furnaces and the coke ovens are cleaned and used as a fuel elsewhere within the works.

DOCK CRANES

As ships get bigger they need more depth of water. The answer at Port Talbot was to build breakwaters out into the sea, creating a tidal harbour away from the shoreline, with a row of 40 tonne gantry-grab cranes along a central servicing jetty.

THE CRUCIBLE

Iron and steel production in south Wales has always been in a constant state of flux as evolving technology brought advantages of cost and efficiency. Prior to 1750, iron was manufactured in small charcoal furnaces that utilised nearby timber and water. When coal became the source of fuel, users quickly realised that different seams offered different burning qualities which determined the cost of operating a furnace. The distance between the iron processing plant and the source of coal was also a critical factor and so works were established where transport factors could be minimised. South Wales produced 40% of all British pig iron by 1830. The sophistication of the blast furnace and the puddling process constantly impacted on the shape and size of the industry with bigger, integrated units offering economies of scale. The application of the Bessemer converter in the second half of the 19th century meant a move towards bigger, continuous process plants.

For a sense of the technology and geography, see 'Welsh Steel' by Robert Protheroe-Jones and the Association of Industrial Archaeology's 'Powerhouse of Industry' Guide.

MARGAM

There are three junctions marked Port Talbot, yet none for Margam, though this is where the steel works lie, on land that was once the Margam estate.

There could be no greater contrast between two sides of a motorway than here: the heaviest of heavy industry across the road from woodland and parks.

The fourth Baron Mansel of Margam had no offspring, so he gave the estate to his sister's son, Thomas Talbot, who hated his inherited house and had it demolished. No gratitude, the young people of the 1770s.

BROMBIL FARM (E.O.)

The green outbuilding is all we can see of a farm once occupied by the Llewellyn family, land agents to the Talbots. When not managing the Margam estate, some served with distinction in the Royal Navy, earning the honour of a personal visit from Lord Nelson. And he stopped over.

WATCH YOUR SPEED

Segments of the Network Q Rally of Great Britain are staged in these parts. It's mostly an off-road affair, but to get between sections, the drivers use normal roads. A police officer decided to monitor the movement of the rally cars along a 30mph stretch of road and recorded a succession of infringements that resulted in Port Talbot magistrates disqualifying 4 participants from driving on British roads for 12 months, 57 penalty points being issued and fines of £7,350 being imposed.

DYFFRYN COMPREHENSIVE

The 13 – 16 year olds attend here, and few find the noise of the motorway a problem. Double-glazing only arrived 5 years ago. Most famous pupil: Richard Burton. How about that for an old boy!

NEATH PORT TALBOT COLLEGE

One site of an institution with 15,000 students, of whom more than 3,000 are full time, taking 40 different subjects at A level between them. It's one of the largest colleges in Wales, with a Remploy award for employing people with disabilities.

ANDREW SCOTT

This building and civil engineering firm has been going since 1870. From these offices they manage construction contracts right across Wales. Their gear is kept a few miles further north on the Baglan Industrial Estate next to Manderwoods.

BLAST FURNACES No 4 AND No 5

This handsome pair combine to produce almost 5 million tonnes of liquid iron each year. In its molten state the mineral is at a terrifying temperature of 1,100 degrees Centigrade. Water sprays are used to reduce the heat. The end product is slabs of steel ready for rolling. Furnace No 4 is the one to the north, that our picture, taken from near the motorway, shows to the right.

SLABBING BAY

Hot steel slabs are rolled into coil. If they haven't come straight from the furnaces they have to be reheated. Behind the slabbing bay is one of the site's two big gasholders.

RADAR STATION (W.O.)

On the top of Graig Fawr are the remnants of a WW2 home chain site dedicated to guarding the Bristol Channel from enemy ships and submarines.

The spot provides a superb view of the steel works (see Page 95).

To get here, park near the Stones Museum off Junction 38 and walk along the tarmac lane towards the back of Margam Castle. Take the second marked footpath left up the ridge, alongside the stone wall. Don't try to do what we did – climb up the face of the hill. It's horribly dangerous.

CAPEL MAIR AR Y BRYN (W.O.)

This outbuilding of the Cistercian Abbey that lay below was where those not worthy of the Abbey could worship. But that all became academic following the dissolution of the monasteries in 1536. Then these 26 acres were bought by Rice Mansel and later became part of the Mansel Talbot empire until the Evans-Bevans picked it up for a snip in auction in 1941.

STONES MUSEUM

Lots of ancient carved stones have been gathered from the surrounding area and elegantly presented in this old school building, below Capel Mair ar y Bryn. We were attracted to the Ogham script: series of notches cut into the edge of stones indicating phonetic sounds based on consonant and vowel clusters, like a primitive Morse Code. Next door is the Abbots Kitchen restaurant occupying a building presented to the Parish of Margam by Sir David and Lady Evans-Bevan in 1973; small beer for the Vale of Neath brewery family. Don't miss the wedding snap of the Count and Countess of Mexborough, him a prat in spats; her looking like she's regretting it already.

Margam Crematorium

Since it opened in 1969 (shortly before the motorway arrived) it's become a popular final destination. Well, perhaps that's not quite the way to put it. The catchment area is about 12 miles in radius, with the deceased of Swansea being brought in considerable numbers. In a typical year 1,400 cremations are conducted here.

J39

PORT TALBOT WORKS

From the top of the hill opposite this is what you can see behind the hot rolling shed. The big dark building furthermost away is the basic oxygen steel-making plant, where oxygen is blown into molten iron and so turned into steel. In front of that (with white smoke coming from it) is the caster where the molten steel is cast into slabs. The chimney on the right in the foreground serves the re-heat furnaces.

The site, that came into being in 1902, was known as the Abbey Works of the Steel Company of Wales, then it became part of British Steel, and now it's Corus Strip Products UK.

The steel manufactured here is supplied to the automotive industry, and used for domestic appliances, racking, ducting, cladding, office furniture and food cans.

COLD ROLL BUILDING

Broad, thick coils of steel are fed into one end of the line and are flattened, sheared, pickled, deoxidised and, as necessary, oiled before coming out the other end, neater and thinner. Some of the product is sold at this stage, the rest goes to Llanwern for further refinement.

MORFA COKE OVENS

These convert coal into coke. There are hopes that a deal may be struck soon with the American Sun Coke firm to build a new £110m heat generation plant that would reduce dependency on imported coke.

COAL HOPPERS

Coal is graded and mixed in these hoppers to feed the Coke Ovens. Ironic that in an area that used to produce a huge proportion of the raw materials for steel-making, most of the iron ore, coal and coke is now imported; though 25% of what goes into the furnaces is scrap steel.

MARGAM COUNTRY PARK (W.O.)

A sailing ship full of citrus plants is wrecked on the shoreline of your huge estate. What do you do? Grab the exotic vegetation and erect an Orangery to impress the neighbours. Then the Mansel Talbots decided to knock up a castle to go with it, with stone from their own Pyle quarry. Come WW2 the government requisitioned the place and stuffed it full of Yanks before D-Day. Now the council keeps what's left in good shape.

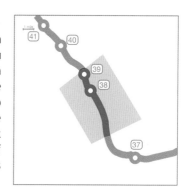

THE PRIORY

This was the clubhouse for the golf course before it was sold off to Dave and Kath, who have turned it into a stylish restaurant that was doing great business when we called. Compelling views of the Corus steel plant lighting up as it gets dark.

KENFIG HOUSE FARM

Brothers Dennis and Anthony Radcliffe run this place, Dennis concentrating on the Black Suffolk sheep, Anthony the beef cattle, that they take to an abattoir in Merthyr or to Ross market. The family have been here since their grandfather returned as an officer from WW1.

TYN CELLAR

These barns, soon to be converted, lie close to a standing stone that is said to walk to the sea for a drink each New Year's Eve.

LAKESIDE GOLF COURSE

You can become a full member for £350 per annum, or take the Pay and Play option for just £6 per round. Oh yeah, but you have to pay £99 a year to do that. If enough people sign up, they'll be able to build a new clubhouse.

J38

BOC (W.O.)

From this plant they supply oxygen, nitrogen, argon, hydrogen and air by pipeline not just to their steel-making neighbours, but also to Knauf Insulation at Cwmbran and other plants in south Wales. They also operate a tanker and cylinder service delivering liquid product as far as Hereford and Swindon. The 25 acre site is the UK's leading centre for the production of synthetic gases.

EGLWYS NUNYDD RESERVOIR

There was an old colliery here, which collapsed in the 1930s creating a big hole that soon filled with water, which became known as the Carbide Pool as it was close to the old Kenfig Carbide works, now demolished. The steel producers turned it into a 250 acre fresh water reservoir. It's now a site of special scientific interest regards its wildlife, and accommodates a sailing club and an angling club, famous for brown trout.

RPC

You know those plastic cups that are supposed to catch the liquid for drinks from vending machines? These silos are full of the stuff that's used to make the cups.
The huge blue building next door is the South Wales Distribution Centre.

KENFIG HILL-MARGAM

This is the Ogmore Vale extension, carrying coal from the Margam open cast site to the freight depot south of the Corus works, for re-distribution to various industrial users in this part of the world.

BORG WARNER

They make wheel assemblies and transmission systems for various car manufacturers. The plant has just won a big contract to supply 4-wheel drive systems for a new Audi sports utility vehicle – yeah, those Chelsea tanks that get through lots of fuel and churn out considerably more pollution than a saloon car.

MARGAM OPENCAST MINE

In March 2005 Celtic Energy distributed a photocopied sheet of A4 paper to local libraries documenting "Answers to some commonly asked questions regarding the extension application:

How big an extension has been applied for? 82 Hectares.

Why is the coal needed? The high quality bituminous coal is unique in Wales. It will continue to be needed to supply existing markets, particularly to Wales's largest Power Station, Aberthaw.

How much coal is involved? 2.4 million tonnes.

How many jobs are involved? The extension would safeguard the 70 well paid jobs.

What about the extra noise and dust? We are currently negotiating with a specialist company regards improvements.

What about the effects of dust on health? Despite several claims to the contrary there is no evidence of any link between opencast coal workings and increased prevalence of respiratory illness or asthma severity in nearby communities."

CARDIFF AIRPORT

Caernarfon is in north Wales near Anglesey. It's a heck of a drive by road to south Wales, as Dafydd, the boss of a small TV production company up there knows. Most of his work came from S4C based in Cardiff, and he, like all producers, had to frequently jump through hoops to keep those commissioners happy – which meant frequent visits to Cardiff, often at short notice.

So he was delighted when he read that a new air service would operate between Caernarfon's airstrip and Cardiff airport. A "suit" soon commanded his presence in Cardiff, so Dafydd phoned the new air route operators and booked a seat on the next morning's flight.

Dafydd turned up at 7 am, briefcase in hand. At the runway office he was pointed to a portakabin, where he found a man studying a map. This was his pilot, who took Dafydd out to a two-seater light aircraft, and asked Dafydd to climb in next to him. Just over an hour later they were in sight of Cardiff Airport, and given instructions to land.

Dafydd asked what time the plane would be returning to Caernarfon. The pilot said: "What time would you like to go?"

Flying back in the evening, the pilot explained that it was much harder to work out where you were in the sky when it was too dark to see the lie of the land. The pilot asked Dafydd to look carefully for a line of lights below, that might be the coast. Dafydd did his best, never having navigated a light aircraft at night before. He kept wondering if they might be horribly near Snowdon. They recognised the straights between the mainland and Anglesey, and so they turned round, doubled back and landed safely.

Cardiff Airport is west of Barry Island and does lots of scheduled and charter flights. It's owned by a Spanish motorway toll company.

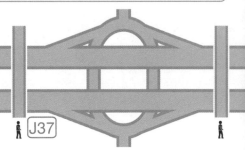

4814

J37

ORION (W.O.)

Mr Masaharu Nakatani is the Managing Director of Orion Electric (UK) Ltd.

They have been making TVs, VHS machines and other domestic electronic devices here on the Kenfig Industrial Estate for the last 20 years. The Universal British Directory of Trade and Commerce of 1790 described the borough of Kenfig as "a straggling place and inhabited by none but farmers, contains about 50 resident and 70 out-dwelling burgesses, each of whom has a vote for the member of the Glamorganshire boroughs".

PYLE-PORT TALBOT

The south Wales mainline leaves the coast and heads eastward inland. First's complimentary magazine had Swansea's Catherine the great (Zeta Jones) on the front cover of its Spring 2005 edition and an article inside about the demanding first year of Managing Director Alison Forster.

ANGEL INN (E.O.)

This place dates back to the 13th century. Inside is popular catering, and while you're waiting for your meal, you can study a fascinating set of panoramic photographs capturing the construction of the viaduct over the River Neath at Briton Ferry in 1950.

Across the road is the base of the cross y ddadl, the cross of debate, where Kenfig burgess disputes were settled – verbally.

ST MARY MAGDALEN, KENFIG (E.O.)

This lies close to a very troubled stretch of coastline where many ships have foundered and where sea floods have swamped the line of the land. Until the late 15th century there was quite a big community here complete with a castle, but it was mostly abandoned after waves of drifting sand devastated the soil.

Pyle

They've got a great library here, than not only records local history but celebrates it too. On a shelf is a length of recovered iron rail from the track of the Duffryn Llynvi and Porthcawl Railway (1825-1860). It commemorates an industrial archaeology project, undertaken by the Kenfig Hill and District Music and Arts Society, studying the first means of export for the early iron and coal industries of the Llynfi and Cynffig valleys. Also on display is a carved lime wood "Box of Dreams" with panels capturing triumphs of the past and aspirations for the future.

STORMY LIME WORKS

This is one of two sites where T.S. Rees refine lime for Corus and other steel plants. There's a fair old bit of scrap metal round the place which makes it look run down, but it's still an active plant that's been going for 20 years.

The name is nothing to do with the weather, but refers to the hamlet down the road.

MAESTEG-BRIDGEND

This single track carries a commuter service up and down the Ogmore valley.

At the start of 2005, a weekly season ticket cost £8.60 for as-many-as-you-like 8 mile rides.

You can stay on the train and go as far as Cardiff, which takes less than half an hour from Bridgend.

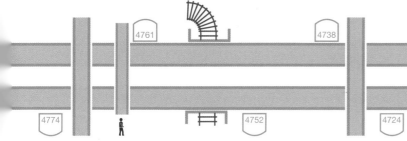

PYLE-BRIDGEND

Peter Strachan, Managing Director of Arriva Trains Wales, regularly evaluates customer comments: "It is clear that punctuality, reliability, security and cleanliness are the topics on which you wish us to focus our attention. Our positive relationship with the Welsh Assembly Government and local authorities continues to deliver real improvements to stations throughout Wales."

RIVER OGMORE

This is draining a catchment area of 272 square kilometres, the Ogmore itself rising north of Maesteg and coming through that town. In 1944 the centre of Bridgend was very seriously flooded. In the 1990s the National River Authority committed substantial efforts to tackling "intermittent pollution and habitat degradation". The western side of the richly-textured Bridgend Circular Walk passes under the M4 here.

MCARTHUR GLEN

This doesn't sound like a Welsh place, and it isn't. They describe it as a designer outlet village, but essentially it's just a corridor of shops adjacent to a giant car park. And it immediately explains why the town centre of Bridgend is so lean and fragmented. All the spending money in the area disappears into this place. Okay, it provides jobs for shop assistants and security guards, but essentially it's sucking money out of Bridgend and into distant organisations.

Porthcawl

How refreshing it was to reach the sea, surf and sun on a delightful Spring afternoon. We walked the well-appointed prom, and got a tea at the Sidoli kiosk. The tide was out, so we could appreciate the rocks and pools. We managed to negotiate a fine sea view room at the Westcliffe, and have an enjoyable supper at the new Waterfront diner. We admired the well-protected harbour with a restored sample of rail track in situ (as detailed in Pyle library).

And we could see big ships in the Bristol Channel with the north coast of Somerset beyond. If we'd had more time we might have invested in lessons at the Simon Tucker Surfing Academy.

SARN PARK SERVICES

Here we find Civic Rescue, which sounds like a spin-off from the Thunderbirds. Every year their 18 trucks (generally acting on behalf of the AA or RAC) attend to around 10,000 breakdowns on and off the motorway between Cardiff and Carmarthen.

"It's not just a lorry with a hook on the back," explained Des Thomas. We look after people and try to deal with their problems, which might be a need for insulin injections or getting back to Scotland in a hurry." They've helped all sorts of nice and interesting people, including Jeremy Irons and an Indian Prince.

On the slipways on and off Junction 36 you pass over a cattle grid, there to stop stray sheep reaching the carriageway.

Maesteg

Here they rightly celebrate the life and achievements of Eisteddfod Gold Medal winner "Cadrawd", Thomas Christopher Evans (1846-1918), of nearby Llangynwyd. His award was for invaluable research into Welsh place names.

The quality and dignity of the roaming (in 2005, based in Bangor) annual arts events are close to inexplicable to the English, who find peak-time Saturday evening TV shows on S4C devoted to Welsh folklore and song completely beyond comprehension.

COUNTY BOROUGH OF BRIDGEND

Looking ahead, they've published a draft community vision for the years 2012 to 2016. Amongst the aims are "a vibrant economy, sustainable development with reduced dependence on the private car, the elimination of ageism, public services available to all, and ensuring it's a healthy place to live, work and visit."

ROCKWOOL FACTORY

This is the UK base for a Danish firm that produce insulation material. What's Rockwool? Well, it's wool made of rock. Such fibres were first discovered close to an Hawaiian volcano – tufts of mineral hair that formed when lava flow cooled in the wind. A Danish scientist reproduced the phenomena in a laboratory by heating volcanic rock to 1,500 degrees Centigrade, then spinning the emerging flow of liquid rock.

EWEENY RIVER

This comes from north of Pencoed, drifts past the Ford engine factory in Bridgend, then joins the Ogmore just before it reaches the sea.

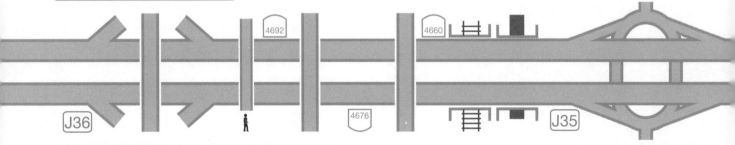

J36 · 4692 · 4660 · 4676 · J35

ODEON

Next to the multi-screens are multi fast food counters, the environment enhanced by giant plastic fruit suspended from the ceiling, implying a world of greengrocery rather than instant synthetic gratification. When we called, it was packed with happy families, some of whom looked like they should concentrate more on fruit and veg.

TOLL TIMES

Back in 1843 the Bridgend Turnpike Trust was much absorbed by policy matters. The Committee conceived that "if it were possible to collect every Toll, every person who makes use of the Roads should pay proportionably for that use, and for the injury done to the Roads, but as it is quite impossible to ascertain the distance for which each individual uses the Road, or to make a graduated scale of Tolls according to the weight carried, an approximation to the object should be attained by placing Gates in such positions as to compel all persons who travel along the Roads to pay at reasonable intervals."

PONTYCLUN-BRIDGEND

This is the Swansea-Cardiff mainline, with hourly services through the main part of the day. Some west-bound services continue on to Pembroke Dock, Milford Haven and Fishguard, for ferry connections to Ireland.

Oh, yeah, and it's a great way to get to Tenby by public transport.

A&E

In the event of you needing emergency medical attention near here, you are directed to the Princess of Wales Hospital in Bridgend, opened by Diana on 11th June 1986. We popped in for a look on the day after the Prince of Wales got married again. We asked if there were any plans to re-name it the Camilla Parker-Bowles Hospital, and were swiftly assured this wouldn't happen.

TAFF ELY WIND FARM

There are 20 of these Danish turbines on towers 35 metres high, with blades of 37 metres diameter, capable of turning at 30 revs per minute and so producing up to 9 megawatts of electricity, which is 22 million kilowatts annually - sufficient to supply 5,500 homes and thus save on 20,000 tonnes of carbon dioxide and 300 tonnes of acid rain entering the atmosphere from a conventional power station.

LLOYDS TSB CONTACT CENTRE

Currently recruiting: "If you enjoy working in a friendly and relaxed environment where professionalism and customer focus are key" you could become a Customer Service Advisor. Minimum of 12 months experience with good all round communication and keyboard skills. Salary £11,700 Pro Rata (£6.43 per hour).

SONY

This is one of two Sony plants in the area. They make professional broadcast cameras and digital TV receivers here. It's also a production site for colour TV sets, but these are on the decline because of the fast-growing appeal of flat screen technology. Literally, on the day we went to press, we heard this place is to close with the loss of 600 jobs.

LLANILID CHURCH

Edward Rice Swan Morgan (1870-1935), third son of a rector, is remembered as "mathematician, linguist, scholar, author, teacher, distinguished for his great ability, unusual originality, the beauty of his life and person."

Pen-coed

The brickworks were the source of prestigious building material for Birmingham's late Victorian municipal frontages. But in 1900 the clay diggers struck a spring which flooded the pits and they never recovered. The Pencoed Foundry became the next big local employer. In the 1920s over 100 men were making 100 coal mine trucks or trams each week.

The Thomas family lorded over the manor for many generations, then cleared off to Canada taking the stained glass windows from their swanky Tregroes House with them. The last in line, Winifred, died off some years ago and local historians managed to retrieve some of her artefacts which are displayed in the charming local library.

Bridgend

During the Second World War over 30,000 local women worked in Royal Ordnance Factory 53. After the war, the site became the home of Kieft Racing Cars, one of which was driven by Stirling Moss in the 1951 Luxembourg Grand Prix. And Bridgend gave the world of rugby one of its most distinguished players, Doctor J. P. R. Williams, who must have wished the M4 had opened earlier, with the number of trips he made between here and Twickenham in the early 1970s. Trivial pursuit answer: John Peter Rhys. We were quite shocked at the state of the town centre, which seemed to lack a focus and a shape and much sense of civic presence. Only later when we got to McArthur Glen did we appreciate that Bridgend has been mugged, and left in a heap at the side of the road by the big, brassy bully on the hill.

ST MARY'S GOLF CLUB

This was until recently the base for a leading Welsh golfer, John Peters. A member of the Welsh amateur team, he has won the Welsh Open, and triumphed in the Pro-Am at Celtic Manor in 2004. He's moved on to become Head of the Golf Academy at the Jack Nicholas course in Llanelli.

There's an 18 and a 12 hole course here, with a 24 room hotel at the back.

Local rule: The Bird Sanctuary behind the 7th hole is out of bounds.

Rhondda

You can by-pass most of south Wales by staying on the M4, and you can skirt round most of the communities in the valleys by utilising the excellent spider's web of trunk roads probably designed to encourage businesses to locate in these areas, but we recommend you get off the motorway and get off the trunk roads and meander in and out of the towns and villages and check out the shops, pubs and cafes, and get a feel for the places and meet the people, not least the cheerful, charming citizens of Rhondda. Rhondda Cynon Taff Council is at the top of the tree regards providing good footpaths and other rights of way.

Rhondda Heritage Park

The most emotive element of an elaborate tour through the facilities and workings of the Lewis Merthyr pit heads was an audio-visual presentation finely narrated by Neil Kinnock about the circumstances and character of the local people. In the art gallery we were fortunate to see Martin Evans's colourful, stylised images of valley buildings, including the Park itself.

You can get here by train from Cardiff. Ask for Trehafod.

OUR PRINTERS

HSW Print (who do our Motorway Sights Guides) are based north of here, off the A4119 at the Clydach Vale Industrial Park, on the site of the Tonypandy colliery, where Winston Churchill sent troops to bluntly suppress demonstrating miners in 1910.

As well as many commercial projects, HSW do hard-back books that are a log of Royal Naval frigate trips. The first in the series was for HMS Cardiff.

Tonypandy's a delightfully distinctive town with lots of individual businesses.

SLATE SIGNS

On Pontyclun's richly textured Cowbridge Road we liked a smart place that does inscribed signs. The slate comes from the Llanberis Pass, and they can provide it in a wide range of shades and finishes.

GWYNFOR EVANS 1913-2005

As we conducted our research in these parts we were struck by the sombre newspaper headlines noting the death of this devoted campaigner for Wales and the Welsh language. Born in Barry, he was educated at Aberystwyth and became President of Plaid Cymru in 1945. In 1980, he threatened to go on hunger strike if Margaret Thatcher didn't approve a Welsh language TV service.

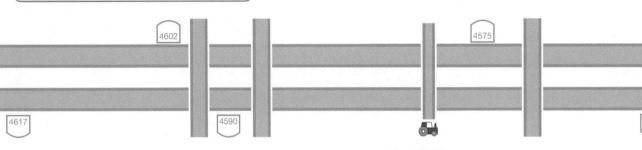

4602   4575

4617   4590   4561

BRIGAM FARM (W.O.)

Dave Williams has recently bought this place from Pencoed College's agriculture department, and is experimentally growing 8 acres of willows as part of a nation-wide assessment project by the Institute of Grassland and Environmental Research, who are studying the practicalities of acquiring sustainable heat and power from short rotation coppice.

VALLEYWOOD

Sir Richard Attenborough has been talking up plans to create a new film studio in these parts. We thought there were already more than enough film studios in Britain, and if there is an need for another, surely better to gut one of those massive buildings at Duffryn Gate?

FOREST WOOD QUARRY

This is operated jointly by Hansons and RMC. It's been going for 50 years and had a new dust-controlling plant installed in 1998 for efficient, environmentally-more-friendly limestone crushing. They use explosives to break up the rock about once a fortnight. That allows them to turn out 1,500 tonnes a day, taken away in 20 tonne loads. When we visited they had gone for 2,051 days without an accident.

ST HILARY TV MAST

A classic analogue transmitter providing a foot-print across a couple of valleys.

Of course, analogue is soon to be switched off, and despite our long experience in the TV industry, we still can't work out how this is in anyone's interests, except for the manufacturers of new TV sets and digital boxes – some of whom are based here in south Wales. Oh, yes.

MISKIN MANOR

Here's somewhere in which the traditional barriers of "them and us" no longer apply. A few generations back you had to be a top nob to get near this place, where the knighted gentry entertained Royalty. Now Mr and Mrs Rosenberg welcome you to enjoy the glories of the premises. If you are able to invest in a £5 lunch time sandwich, you can sit and contemplate the same stag's head-adorned wood-panelled walls that an heir to the throne once mused upon. Then in the Gents they try to seduce you into a return visit: "Looking for 'Brownie Points' with the wife? Why not a candlelit dinner for that anniversary, birthday or just celebration of being together? Choose one of our four-poster suites for a truly romantic time. And we'd all be happy."

RIVER ELY

This starts life near the Taff Ely Wind Farm and meanders its way to join the Taff at its mouth just north of the lovely Victorian town of Penarth, where the Editor had his happiest childhood year attending the Grammar School.

Llantrisant

A proud and dignified community on the top of a hill. Explore the traditional toy shop and the Bull Ring General Store. (Bull baiting was stopped in 1827 because of the unruly nature of the huge crowds). And make sure you get inside the excellent Model House craft design centre (closed on Mondays). We liked Eve Tarver's recycled rubber and plastic garden decorations. Outside is Peter Nicholas's engaging 1982 statue to unconventional inhabitant Dr William Price (1800-1893) surgeon, Chartist and "self-styled" Druid.
The Lord Mayor of London of 1892 came from here, and popped back in his civic robes and gold chain so his fellow natives could see how well he'd done.

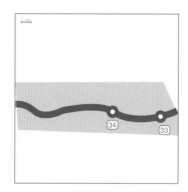

CARDIFF WEST SERVICES

We met two motorway patrol officers on their break in here. The message they wished to convey to drivers was: Use Lane 1. Far too many people sit in the middle lane unnecessarily, forcing all passing vehicles to manoeuvre to the outside lane. The Headquarters of the South Wales Police is an impressive civic building on the southern outskirts of Bridgend.

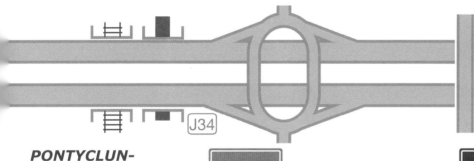

J34

J33

PONTYCLUN-CARDIFF

This is the south Wales mainline, which, at the start of the 20th century was carrying around 100 trains a day, all travelling at different speeds - quite a timetabling challenge.

Barry

Local publishers Vale and Valley produced a fascinating book a few years ago capturing the changes to the town, both visually and anecdotally. It's a big coffee table affair with excellent photographs old and new, exposing the evolving environment. And it's peppered with pithy observations by local people reflecting on what life was like, and how it could be better, both now and in the future. Distinctive and engaging.

Cardiff Bay

We bow to the audacity of creating a barrier across the mouth of the Taff and Ely to create a stable lake, which, when they've sorted out a few scrappy patches, you'll be able to walk right round, exploring all sorts of interesting things on the way.

Museum of Welsh Life

There's a fantastic collection of superbly restored buildings on this site, with exquisite interiors that include real fires in the hearths. Plus a marvellous cross-section of artefacts in the galleries, ranging from a row of old carved wooden harps to the 'Cool Cymru' mini-dress that helped draw tabloid newspaper attention to the launch of the Welsh Assembly.

Barry Island

A by-product of the determination to ship steam coal (for powering steam ships) out of south Wales was the development of holiday services on Barry Island that could be reached by the rail lines laid to carry coal trains. Now you can visit the steam railway, and the up-to-date amusement park, just down the line, where a Butlins used to be.

Penarth

In 1905 the Council advertised the place as "the Pride of the Principality, with unrivalled attractions to the Holiday-maker, Tourist or Persons seeking An Ideal Place of Residence with diversified scenery of Sea and Landscape, a Well-Designed Esplanade and Pier, Handsome Public Buildings and Splendid Docks crowded with Shipping." One hundred year later, it hasn't changed much, apart from the docks which are now a marina.

DE COURCEY'S

You can get married here, but if it's on a summer Saturday you must turn up with at least 80 guests for the reception. It's £700 to hire the Tapestry Room. A 3-course meal is from £29.50, evening buffet from £14.95 per person.

House wines from £14 a bottle, champagne at £6.25 a glass. They throw in use of their silver cake knife, but the Bride and Groom are responsible for any damage.

Merthyr Tydfil

We came here with the Rural Media Company to interview Carol Davies and John Bibby, designated teachers responsible for children in care, for a training video for the Who Cares Trust 'Believe in Me' project. The two teachers were chosen nationally to exemplify good practice, and it was a privilege to see how they kindly and diplomatically handled troubled youngsters living apart from their parents.

RIVER TAFF

This comes down through Merthyr and is joined by the Rhondda at Pontypridd before reaching Cardiff.

Canoeists paddle down 10 km of it in two and a half hours, avoiding the occasional shopping trolley and making sure they get out before Trefforest, below which the weir is "lethal". Upstream, try to track down the extraordinary 1866 15-arched Cefn Viaduct 30 metres high and 200 metres long.

CASTEL COCH

When you've got more money than sense, why not have a fancy folly erected in the country, to give you and your neighbours a change of scene. That's what Lord Bute decided to do and this was where he did it. Yeah, looks all wrong, doesn't it. Nothing like a Welsh castle, more like something out of a pantomime. And inside it's also distinctly theatrical, with some absurd proportions, especially in the bedrooms, by which we mean the size of the furniture. Bet all his friends told him it was fab.

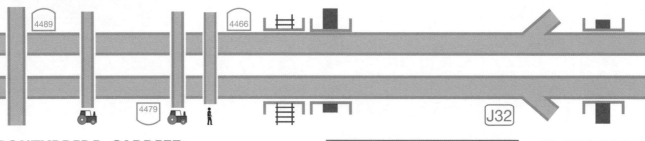

PONTYPRIDD-CARDIFF

This is the spine of the old Taff Valley Railway as recorded enthusiastically in D.S. Barrie's Oakwood Press book: "A story of pioneer enterprise in a land awakened to vast changes and sweeping progress; a story of vigorous expansion, of hard times, of fierce and almost uncontrolled competition, of prosperity well-nigh fantastic; and ultimately of the submergence of local automony in a vast national industry." It opened in 1840, a first class ticket from Cardiff to Merthyr 5 shillings, second class 4 shillings and third class 3 shillings.

GE HEALTHCARE

These people produce medical diagnostic equipment, some of which utilise radioactive isotopes. In the past, whilst the Environment Agency has permitted certain levels of discharge from the site into the air or water, local lobby groups have raised health questions about the plant, previously known as Amersham. Tritium has traditionally been an element of the production process, and it's believed that exposure to certain densities could cause a statistically significant risk of ill-health. The firm say they operate well inside recommended guidelines.

GLAMORGAN-SHIRE CANAL

This opened in 1798 to provide a link between the Merthyr Tydfil iron works and Cardiff (dropping 568 feet along its 25 miles). Now it forms part of a nature reserve that includes the Longwood Site of Special Scientific Interest, listed in the Glamorgan Inventory of ancient woodlands as a river terrace woodland of great antiquity; semi-natural broad-leaved woodland with oak and ash standards dominating the southern section and beech standards to the north.

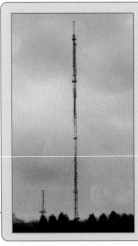

CULVERCROSS MAST

This pumps pictures out from what was HTV Wales, once a regional powerhouse of ITV. They did things like Robin of Sherwood. Sadly, like most regional ITV companies it's now a shadow of its former self, doing just a few local heritage and crime programmes, that look like Panorama next to the network's starlets screaming at snakes in Australian media compounds.

GREENMEADOW SPRINGS

Yes, they do look more like offices, don't they!

Closest to the carriageway is the headquarters of Pathway Care, an independent fostering service, who, in 2004, organised the fostering of over 350 children.

They provide a service for local authorities who are overwhelmed with need for care parenting for children. Set up in 1996, they are now one of the largest private care providers in south Wales.

COED-Y-WENALLT

BT's is the biggest of a little forest of masts that sits in the middle of a little forest that is on the only tract of real upland in Cardiff. The hillside is composed of carboniferous limestone, red marl brownstone and quartz conglomerate. Wenallt means 'white height' and this name probably derives from the fact that the area was once thick with a sea of silver birch.

Currently the shrub cover includes alder buckthorn (Latin: Frangula alnus) and this provides a valuable breeding habitat for the brimstone butterfly.

JUNCTION 31?

No, you haven't missed one, and neither have we. There isn't one - yet!

But who knows what lies ahead. Plans are afoot to lay a third lane in each direction along here, as the next measure to deal with the rapidly increasing density of traffic.

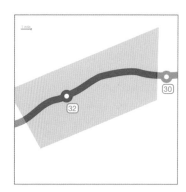

CAERPHILLY-CARDIFF

This is a commuter line that heads up the Rhymney Valley – once it has reached the Valley. Construction of the route (originally, like most of the railways round here, designed to traffic steam coal to the coast, and ore to iron works) required a daunting one-mile long tunnel north of this point to get beyond the Llanishen ridge.

SOUTH WALES TRAFFIC MANAGEMENT CENTRE

One of two operational bases for the Transport Directorate of the Welsh Assembly Government, monitoring and managing 150 km of motorway, 700 km of dual carriageway and 2,000 km of trunk roads, using cameras and detection devices, and then feeding relevant information on to variable message signs and other media.

THE STEAM COAL MUST GET THROUGH

The coal from the Welsh valleys was the best stuff in the world for fuelling the boilers of the Royal Navy, and it was shipped across oceans to meet their needs.

During the First World War, when much of the fleet was positioned north of Scotland around Scapa Flow, the naval suppliers turned to trains to get the fuel through. For several months in 1916, every day of the week at least 15 coal trains of 40 eight ton wagons carried Welsh steam coal northward to Grangemouth for ferrying out to Admiral Jellicoe's vessels; in all, 5.5 million tons.

Cardiff

It's big, it's bustling and it's full of confidence. As a city it's 100 in 2005, and for 50 years it's been the Capital of Wales. It's where the Welsh Assembly is based, which keeps behaving in ways that makes English government look stuck in tramlines. There is a full complement of fine stone civic buildings, and a fine array of popular facilities for shopping, eating and drinking.

The old coal port is now a formidable waterfront. They've got the Millennium Stadium - that has dug English football out of its black hole that was Wembley. And now there's the Millennium Arts Centre too, that opened in November 2004 and has already platformed a spectrum of entertainment from Max Boyce to the Welsh National Opera, and in its first summer will embrace the Urdd National Eisteddfod. We like the cheerful catering at the Norwegian Church Arts Centre and the compelling scale model of the bay area in the Tube Visitor Centre.

Cardiff was once the world's biggest coal exporting dock, main beneficiary of which was the third Marquis of Bute, who blew bits of his mountain of money on tarting up the medieval castle into a Victorian party venue.

DUTCH NURSERY

Jaap Deen came to England nearly 30 years ago to learn the language, and stayed. His place is delightfully unlike your average garden centre. For a start everything's much better value: heaps of plants shipped over from Holland at £2 a pot. Wood chippings at £2 a bag (you shovel them in yourself from a mountain of tree surgeon shreddings), and fire wood at £5 a car full. He holds 100 varieties of trees and has an evolving display of the giant wood carvings of John Hobbs.

Jaap also has strong views on motoring politics and thinks there should be a Park and Ride facility here to take pressure off Cardiff commuting.

CEFN MABLY COUNTRY PARK

Doesn't sound so good in translation: Mable's Ridge.

The big house (which was a Royalist stronghold back in the English civil war) was acquired by Courtney, Lord Tredegar in 1924, simply so he could get his hands on the hunting in the surrounding forests. He handed the house over to the health authorities who turned it into a sanatorium for tuberculosis (for which there was patently no shortage of patients from the pits). That closed in 1984. It was empty for 10 years and then suffered a fire.

Now it's swanky apartments in a secure compound. Isolation of a different kind. But nice Farm Park open to all nearby.

A 48 M

This runs south-west towards the centre of Cardiff. Once it stops being motorway it passes the enormous University Hospital of Wales, a vast complex of both patient care and specialist expertise. As you head from the busy, friendly lobby to the wards, take a moment to appreciate the huge painting of Aneurin Bevan, without whom so much of the social fabric of the UK might not have so successfully come into being.

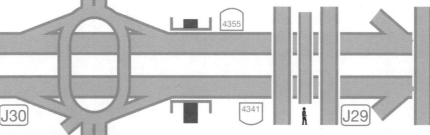

4355 | J30 | 4341 | J29

HBOS CARD SERVICES

You know those credit cards you wish you didn't have. Well, this is where they do some of the sobering sums that appear on those statements. HBOS stands for Halifax Bank of Scotland. They got into bed together in 2001 to give themselves 22 million customers and recent annual profits of £3.8 billion.

RHYMNEY RIVER

This is the western-most of four almost parallel rivers running from the edge of the Brecon Beacons toward the mouth of the Severn. (The others west to east are the Sirhowy, the Ebbw and the Lywd.) Get up to Hengoed by train or the A472 to see the stunning railway viaduct over the Rhymney. The river does a sharp east at Caerphilly before swinging south again near here. The waters service the extensive nurseries just visible to our north.

DUFFRYN GATE

In winter you can see the top of this. It sits across the A48, marking an arrival in Newport's own silicon valley.

The massive white structures to the south are part occupied by Korean firm, LG Electronics, who turned out millions of TVs, but recently downsized because of the market move towards flatscreen. This meant layoffs, and the repayment to the Welsh Government of £35m of the set-up grants they had utilised in establishing their operations here.

CARDIFF GATE SERVICES

Slightly Euro-flavour here with an Ibis French motel on site.
There are nearly 50 Ibis premises in the UK and they mostly employ French staff, learning English.
To get you in the mood, the Total petrol station's called 'Bonjour'.

Caerphilly

They like to think they are a cut above the rest round here, we were told. It may be something to do with their proximity to a great big castle (a similar syndrome to the one that affects some of the citizens of Windsor over at Junction 6). Caerphilly Castle is so large you'd be hard pressed to fit more than a couple of them into the Wilko site at Newport. We were taken with the Edwardian-style waitresses in Glanmor's tea rooms, providing excellent views of magnificent ramparts. And only Caerphilly can lay claim to having given the world Tommy Cooper.

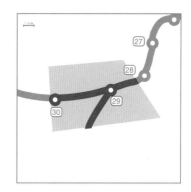

UP VALLEY, DOWN VALLEY

By way of contrast to the glories of Cardiff and to appreciate how the luxuries of life here were funded, when in Blaenavon (for your compulsory journey into a coal mine – see Page 31), check out the remains of the iron works and the town streets and see how utilitarian it all is between the ecclesiastical and civic buildings. There's a magnificent Workmen's Hall that sometimes functions as a cinema, a delightful 1930s Post Office, and an admirable cluster of second-hand book shops that we were told are in coalition with Hay-on-Wye. But you nevertheless gain a sense of the gritty functionalism that constituted life here whilst the burgers of the capital enjoyed their prosperity.

Risca

Not that many years ago there was a chronically high level of unemployment here and the place was badly run down, but things are distinctly picking up, and the atmosphere along the main street opposite the green seemed very healthy when we visited.

J.H.A Roberts's assessment, in 'A View from the Hill', records that the first council houses of the district were completely renovated in the years 1982 to 1985 to bring them up to modern standards. "They were equipped with the now obligatory bathrooms, indoor toilets and central heating."

Do we detect a note of disapproval?

One lady told us too many new houses were now being built. The old Palace Picture Theatre is a listed building and will be soon done up. And she was looking forward to the railway line reopening.

KILSBY & WILLIAMS

These chartered accountants "exist to serve privately-owned businesses, the entrepreneurs that run them and those who have successfully generated private wealth." Taxation services include Corporate, Personal, Inheritance, Capital Gains, Value Added and investigations. They also run a financial advice arm that addresses "wealth preservation."

CERTUS IT (W.O.)

They "provide integrated managed services and support combining enterprise level systems management"... and so on. To be frank, we were much more intrigued by the occupants of Clampett House round the back, who do "90 second showrooms." What on earth could they be? Yeah, we should have found out, shouldn't we!

ACORN

This is headquarters of a recruitment agency and training provider that has half-a-dozen branches in Wales and several in English cities. They've been growing for ten years and altogether employ 250 people at their offices, helping others get jobs or upgrade.

HEART STOPPING

An ambulance driver in a Ford Sierra Cosworth was stopped by the police after doing 148 mph along here. He was transporting a heart to save a child's life in Oxford, so he got off with a caution.

Under the 1984 Road Traffic Regulations, ambulance drivers transporting patients, as well as the Police and fire engines, are exempt from speed limits, but vehicles carrying blood and human organs are not included, and so have to obey restrictions.

USKMOUTH POWER STATION (E.O.)

This is a switch on/switch off/switch on again sort of plant, at Nash on the eastern peninsula of the mouth of the Usk. It has suffered from technological change and the evolving price of electricity. Originally a coal-burning facility employing 2,000 workers, it proved to be inefficient so was mothballed in the 1990s. Another operator bought it up and re-fitted it, bringing it back on stream in the year 2000, to provide the National Grid with 360 megawatts of power. The stack is 122 metres high, and the plant now has a desulphurisation unit to cleanse what comes out of it.

Festival Park

It's a 'factory shopping village' just south of Ebbw, with a woodland craft centre and owl sanctuary alongside. On your way, pop into the Vale villages to support little local shops and get a sense of the community culture.

Forest Drive

Just 5 miles from the motorway is the Welsh Forestry Commission run Cwmcarn Forest, well equipped with visitor facilities. You can drive, bicycle or stroll through miles of richly textured woodland. Or for those who like excitement: "testing climbs, swooping descents and demanding technical sections." What is it? The Twrch mountain bike track – named after the famous wild boar of Mabinogion legends.

RIVER EBBW

Probably the most well-known of the rivers running down the south Welsh valleys; this one of course from Ebbw Vale, running into the Usk close to its mouth, south of Newport Docks. Parts of the beautiful valley reminded us of the Lake District. All the steel works structures have been completely removed.

Cwmbran

This place seems out of place in Wales because it has the feel of a provincial English town centre – stuffed full of chain store branches along its malls. It is Wales's only new town, and, if car park density is a measure, then immensely popular. The horizon is dominated by the tallest tower block in the country at 22 floors and the chimney of the Knauf Insulation works. We preferred the harmonious natural world of the Greenmeadow Community Farm down the road.

RISCA-PILLGWENLLY

Passenger services ended in 1962, then freight services stopped when Corus closed Ebbw Vale steel works in 2002, but now there are admirable plans to commence a new passenger service from Ebbw to Cardiff.

High Cross

In this expanded village we find the Fourteen Locks Canal Centre manned enthusiastically by the Monmouthshire Brecon and Abergavenny Canals Trust.

MONMOUTH CANAL CRUMLIN ARM

Opened in 1799, but effectively replaced by a rail line 25 years later. To the south of the carriageway you can see the line of the towpath dropping eastward as it descends towards the Malpas Junction where it joins with the main Newport to Brecon length.

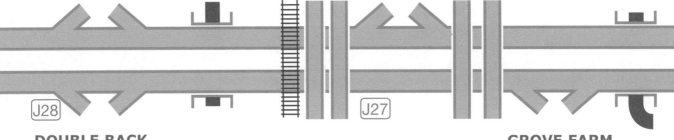

J28   J27

DOUBLE BACK

Our carriageway is ruthlessly straightened so it heads uniformly west-east – a unique contrivance without which these Guides would not work. The brutality of our geographical manipulation is exposed here if you examine the Mini-map in the top right corner of Page 31. The true track of the M4 swings round so that briefly the eastbound carriageway is heading west and vice versa.

PATENT OFFICE (W.O.)

The Open Government Liaison Officer admitted to us that this is the place where records are kept regarding Copyright, Designs, Patents and Trade Marks. The building houses the Intellectual Property and Innovation Directorate. So if you have a brainwave for a new invention, this is the place to register it.

GROVE FARM

Marian Strickland's been looking after animals for 35 years here, and been running kennels and a cattery for 12 years. Typical stay for a dog is a week, prices ranging from £6 to £9 a night dependent on size. When we called she had three labradors in for a month because their Swansea owners' house had been flooded. The longer the dogs stay, the more they like it, as they get used to the routines.

Tredegar House

See how the other half lived. Except it wasn't half. More like half of one per cent – the Morgans and their like, whose land yielded the timber, coal, limestone and iron ore that others had to hew and haul.

After centuries of living it up, death duties forced the family to hand their ancestral home over the council. Now it's tooled up for public visits and events. In the Orangery is Britain's longest single plank oak tabletop – a 17th century 11 metre shovelboard.

MONMOUTHSHIRE AND BRECON CANAL

The Monmouthshire Canal ran from Newport to Pontypool and the separate Brecknock and Abergavenny Canal offered a service from there to Brecon. This allowed the movement of coal, iron, limestone and lime between industrial sites, and down to Newport Docks. Tram roads conveyed the material from mines to the canals. They functioned from the end of the 18th century and became one company in 1812, carrying vessels 19 metres long by 2.7 metres wide that could take 25 tons. The Great Western Railway took it over and ran it down late in the 19th century.

MALPAS FIRE STATION

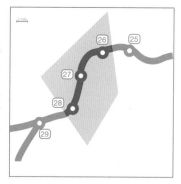

One of 50 stations serving 1.4 million people in south Wales. Overall they have a budget of £60m and 1,700 employees. Last year the service received 69,000 emergency calls and attended 34,000 incidents, of which 21,000 were fires, and 9,000 were false alarms. Of the fires, 7,000 were grass, 6,000 refuse, 3,000 vehicles deliberately set alight, and 1,000 dwellings, where cooking had been the most likely cause.

EURO COMMERCIALS

One of four Welsh bases for a Mercedes truck maintenance and repair business.
A standard 2-hour inspection must be carried out on lorry cabs every 6 weeks regardless of mileage. The firm also install and calibrate Lucas-Kienzle tachographs to all types of trucks. The calibration has to be checked every two years.

J26

Big Pit

For anyone who has come across the Severn estuary into Wales for the first time, a visit here should be compulsory, because it abruptly conveys an impression of what has determined the nature of this part of the world. Early in the 20th century south Wales produced a third of the world's coal exports, leaving the coast from Cardiff, Swansea, Barry Island and Newport. The remains of this pit at Blaenavon (14 miles to the north) are nothing special. It's just that they are still intact, when 100 years ago there were 2,000 pits, employing 250,000 men, a quarter of the adult male population.

Within a World Heritage Site is this National Mining Museum of Wales, where ex-miners such as Gavin Rogers will take you down the shaft in a cage and lead you through crudely shored up passages explaining how he and his predecessors used to have to hack out coal – under unbelievably terrible conditions. More than 200 men died in this mine. The trip is raw and disconcerting. No Disneyland fibreglass replicas, it's sobering and humbling, and puts everything above ground into perspective.

Just before we went to press it became the Gulbenkian Museum of the Year.

NEW BYPASS?

The M4 is close to capacity in these parts, so the Wales Spatial Plan has given initial consideration to the Trunk Road Forward Programme proposal to build a Toll Motorway from Junction 23 to Junction 29, running south of the city of Newport and through the docks. This would relieve pressure on the existing carriageway, which would mean improvements could be made to it. That would also then allow the application of restrictions on usage of the existing motorway, which might become dedicated to buses, coaches and cars with at least one passenger inside.

Roman Fortress/Remains

Heaps of impressive Roman remains in and around Caerleon. Big chunks of amphitheatre and barracks can be seen, despite a considerable proportion of the houses in the town having been built from what was originally Roman stone work. Endeavours to preserve the relics began in 1850. Archaeologist Sir Mortimer Wheeler persuaded the Daily Mail to sponsor important excavations in the 1920s. We like the Baths where lots of gold rings and chains were found down the drains.

BT, MALPAS

When this place was built in the 1960s, every cubic foot was required to accommodate switching gear, relays and cabling. But technology changes, which usually means it gets smaller. So these days all of Malpas's phone network can be controlled from inside a small box.

BT used to also occupy the building next door to store cables and tools, but that stuff can now fit in here as well.

CHRISTCHURCH, MALPAS

Nothing to do with Christchurch the place. Housed in the old British Telecom stores, it's the UK base for an American family of 63 churches known as the Sovereign Grace Ministries, who describe their doctrine as "being essentially Reformed, yet including a commitment to charismatic practice as biblically defined". They aim to plant new churches "to bring glory and honour to God".

Caerleon

This is a lovely place with more than its share of good pubs, restaurants and cafes - of which we like Maggie Mays in the Ffwrwm (seat) Alley with its wooden sculptures. It's got an Endowed School that dates back to the 1717 will of businessman Charles Williams, who was born here and got very rich in London.

RIVER USK

Rising in the Brecon Beacons and passing through the pleasant town of Usk, this river has one of the most extreme tidal ranges at its mouth:12 metres on occasions.

CWMBRAN-NEWPORT

On the Manchester Piccadilly-Cardiff line with hourly services in both directions.

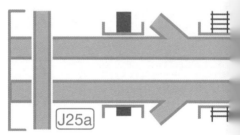

J25a

CRINDAU TUNNELS

Cut between 1961 and 1964 these were the first motorway tunnels in Britain, in essence bringing to fruition the Newport bypass concept devised by road engineer Hugh Jones back in 1944. Some councillors lobbied for six lanes instead of four but were overruled. The approaches necessitated the demolition of 160 houses and shops. As you near the tunnels from the west you can see the Newport Lodge Hotel almost directly above.

CIVIC CENTRE

This 1963 clock tower sits atop the offices of the directors of lifelong learning, corporate services, education-related services, human resources and policy, law and standards and leisure-related services. Also inside are the civic suite, the Council Chamber and the Mayor's Office and Parlour.

BEWATOR

You know those doors that you can't open without a special swipe card or pressing in numbers to a keypad. Maybe you don't, but we come across them a lot in our line of work. Well, they are often supplied by this Swedish firm, who also do video surveillance and other "security" facilities for private companies and places like hospitals where you don't want the patients wandering about in the medicine stores.

STILLS DESIGN

Web/graphics outfit who've moved to Cardiff, but still own this building

R J MASON

Roland Mason has been operating his 30 strong fleet of general haulage trucks from here for 4 years, on the site of where Wynns Heavy Haulage used to be.

Roland likes a broad range of customers so they are not dependent on any particular type of trade. They might take fork lift truck parts to Manchester and bring plastic bottles back.

Christchurch

This hill with a church on top was once owned by a Benedictus Priory at Goldcliff five miles south of here, then became the property of Eton College. And now it's part of the City and County of Newport.

GREENWOOD

Twelve floors on this centrepiece of the St Julian's estate, with a Londis at the bottom, where we met long time local resident Anthony Buller, a gardener. He remembers when the houses were first built here, leaving a channel of greenery that would later become the M4 carriageway. He and his pals played Robin Hood and William Tell there – it was "heavenly". He still observes owls and badgers nearby.

LAWRENCE HILL ALLOTMENTS

Retired truck driver Mike Wardle spends about an hour a day here tending to his eight perch patch. (A perch being 30.25 square yards). Normal price for such an allotment is £20 per annum, but as Mike is a pensioner he gets his for half price, with a little concrete shed thrown in. He and his wife grow enough vegetables to see them through the year and have lots left to give away. The ground is good for broad and runner beans, spuds, sweet corn, carrots, parsnips and cabbage.

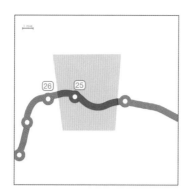

HOLY TRINITY, CHRISTCHURCH (W.O.)

In here is a huge 14th century healing stone. A big slab of inscribed slate on which sickly people would lie in the hope of better health.

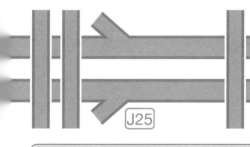

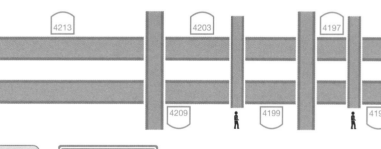

TRANSPORTER BRIDGE

This is a gem of industrial archaeology. 6 cars at 50p a time can be carried on a gondola platform slung on cables beneath a track that runs across the top of the structure. The towers are 74 metres tall and 180 metres apart. It's a French design, which allowed tall ships to sail up and down the river without disruption.

Take a ride across and try to make it when the Visitor Centre is open so you can enjoy the amusing guide. www.newport.gov.uk/transporterbridge for times.

It's the best example of its kind in the world, and will soon reach its centenary: 12th September 2006. All credit to the enthusiasts who have lobbied for its maintenance over the years.

Newport

Pigot's 1835 Directory for Monmouthshire presented an inspiring account of the town: "Finely situate upon the river Usk, over which is an elegant stone bridge. The river is navigable for vessels of large size, has here a very rapid and high tide, and is extremely favourable for an extensive trade, which, indeed, it at this time enjoys. There is much business done in timber, corn and slate; but the export of iron and coal forms the principal trade of Newport, the extent of which may be judged by the following returns: Year 1827: Tons of Iron: 79,781; Tons of Coal 410,138. Year 1834: Iron: 114,355; Coal: 434,414.

The iron and coal are brought down to Newport from the numerous works in the hills, both by canal and railway; the conveyance along the latter being expedited by several locomotive engines. Ship building is now so much pursued here that at this time there are seven vessels on the stocks: for this branch the river is particularly well calculated, as vessels of almost any burthen can be launched from the dock into deep water. That the local advantages of this town have not been lost upon its inhabitants, is evidenced by the improvements which have taken place, both in respect to neatness and extent, and which entitle it to be considered the metropolis of the county. The streets are well paved, and lighted with brilliant gas, for which the coal here is particularly well adapted; and, upon the whole, the general aspect is that of decided prosperity."

CELTIC MANOR RESORT

This is a stonker, isn't it. Talk about an iconic gateway to a new wealthy Wales. It's enormous and audacious and seems like something that would be more at home in Los Angeles

So how come it's here? Well, many years ago, the old Manor House halfway up the hill was a nursing home, and baby Terry Matthews was born there. The lad grew up to be a successful businessman, making a fortune from telecommunications in Canada. So he thought he'd do his bit for the homeland. He bought up the old house and the land around it and developed the hotel and golf courses on a scale that might seem run-of-the-mill in north America. Nice pot of coffee and up-market biscuits for £2.50 in the cavernous luxury bar, which will be full of Ryder Cup competitors in 2010.

COURT FARM

This has been in Roger Lewis's family for many generations. The building dates from the 15th century. Roger's parent's core business was water cress production, until a health scare nationally about the dangers of liver fluke killed it off in the 1960s. Now Roger and his wife, June, run a DIY livery stable, that has occasionally accommodated very successful horses including Hors La Loir II that won the Cheltenham Champion hurdles and Carvill-Shill, which triumphed in the Welsh Grand National at Chepstow. Help yourself to the black horse manure.

OLD BARN

Roger Lewis of Court Farm used one of his own out-buildings to set up a pub and restaurant for the hamlet of Llanmartin in 1988. It's had a succession of landlords since, with mixed results until taken over a year ago by Jackie Pratt who also runs The Ship in Caerleon. She's done the place up and improved the menu and now it's thriving. And in the foyer there's a Community News notice board that features lots of letters of thanks for good meals and enjoyable occasions.

4148

4160

4146

J24

ALCATEL

They produce lots of telecommunications stuff, from mobile phones to trans-oceanic submarine cables. They're big on "global broadband highways", and so everyone in the industry knows what to do next, they operate a university here where customers for their products and services can get bespoke train-ing. So, no wonder hotel prices round here are high, when technicians are turning up from Europe, the Middle East and Africa to find out why e-mails aren't get-ting through when you want them to, and why spam seems to reach you despite all your attempts to stop it.

A BIT DENSE

Too many cars around here, and not enough places to park. To inhibit ad hoc Park and Ride schemes the McDonalds at Junction 24 (opposite an American semi-conductor firm that was twitchy about appearing in our book) have erected a notice that reads: "Car park for McDonald's customer's only. Any car found to be abusing this facility will be clamped and removed at the owners expense." Yes, someone obviously hadn't been referring to their 'Eats, Shoots & Leaves'.

UNDERWOOD

Up high we can see a white gable end indicating a housing estate that has grown in recent years. When they kicked off they had an enterprising community newspaper called the BUSH Telegraph: Bishton and Underwood Self Help.

WELCOME TO THE CITY OF NEWPORT

Now listen up, little ones – yes, you lot who think books are old-fashioned and everything you need to know is on the web. We googled this place and got the Sixth Edition of the on-line Columbia Encyclopedia, which declares that "lumber, tea, automobiles and aircraft are made."

Put that in your exam paper and see what marks you get.

NEWPORT DOCKS

The port's first enclosed dock opened in 1842. Just over one hundred years later the British Transport Commission concluded that "the present docks can justifiably claim to be amongst the most modern in the country both in manner of their layout and in the way they are equipped. Coal is the principal commodity dealt with, from the standpoint of tonnage."

In 1964 Newport stopped exporting coal, and now imports the fuel.

But the dock has a bespoke steel export facility and handles in excess of half-a-million tonnes of steel a year. WE Dowds handle coils using two 25 tonne quayside cranes, two 40-tonne gantry cranes, 28-tonne capacity fork lift trucks and a fleet of 75-tonne capacity trailers.

ST MARTIN, LLANMARTIN

Biggest stone in the graveyard is In loving memory of Edith Decima, beloved daughter of J & L Baker, Wilcrick, who died Dec 10th 1913, aged 29 years.
"Gone from us, but not forgotten, Never shall thy memory fade.
Loving thoughts shall ever linger round the spot where thou art laid".

4141

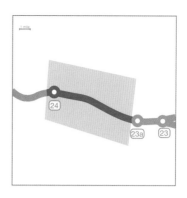

Monmouth

Terrific collection of Lord Nelson artefacts in the Museum. Visiting in 1802, aged 44, with Lady Hamilton, he was "grey, tired, disappointed, with no right arm and a sightless right eye, and was rarely out of pain." But he wrote a scathing report on the lack of Navy timber in the Forest of Dean.
Also intriguing early photos of Charles Rolls (of Royce fame). And try and see a screening in the nearby 1927 Savoy cinema – a trip down memory lane in itself. Until recently you could drive across the ancient bridge over the River Monnow, just before it enters the Wye. Now, sensibly, cars must take a new bridge round the back of the Waitrose car park.

4133

4136

4125

LLANWERN STEEL WORKS (W.O.)

This site functions in conjunction with Port Talbot as Corus Strip Products UK. Slabs of steel are brought by rail from Port Talbot to be both hot and cold rolled here as required. Across a 1,000 acre plant they heat and roll the slabs to form coils. These can then be finished in various ways. From the motorway we can see one end of the works, part of the zinc coating line and the Zodiac galvanising unit. Over 1,000 people work here. Worldwide, Corus has 48,000 employees across 40 countries.

WILKINSON DISTRIBUTION DEPOT

A big silver shed with a red strip along it and containing 12 kilometres of conveyor belts. Who's would that be? Why Wilkinson. 850,000 square feet servicing their 100 odd stores across southern England, the West Midlands and Wales.
When we visited on Good Friday we counted 120 articulated trailers in the compound.
Tescophobs will be disturbed to learn that next door is the superstore's dry goods regional distribution centre, a fifth of a mile long, making the frozen and chilled shed at Chepstow look not much more than a corner shop.

INTERBREW

Fancy a Stella? Got that continental aura to it. You might imagine it's come from somewhere in the middle of Europe. Well, you'd be imagining wrong. Your Artois poured out of this place. And if that wasn't bad enough, Manchester's Boddington Bitter also emerges from here. What you've got to understand is that: "optimisation is based on the results of a capacity-utilisation review to improve cost structure through further optimisation of the existing Western European plant network." Not a micro-brewery then.

35

MAGOR FIRST SERVICES

Hard work running a service area when you don't have economies of scale. But at least it makes things a bit different. We like the big screens in the café showing ever-evolving Traffic Wales road information. First Services also have a petrol station site halfway up the A49. Lots of daffodils on the central reservation of the A49 when we came down it, so we stopped at a florists near here to buy some and were told their daffs came from Lincolnshire.

WINDMILL

(W.O.)
It's on Windmill Lane, with two cottages facing it. One's called Windmill Cottage and the other is Windmill Cottage 2.

IFTON COURT

The west wing was sold off to a couple who undertook considerable home improvements, which led to the council re-assessing the tax band of the properties, moving the original building up a costly notch despite no work having been done to it.

ST MICHAEL'S

John Ansty farms alongside this chapel that closed not long after his daughter was christened 20 years ago. He lost 50 acres to the original M4, and another 50 to the new one here at Llanvihangel.

ST MARY'S, ROGIET

Now an outpost of the parish of Portskewett. When the church had dedicated rectors they lived at Ifton Court, and one built a scale model of Portskewett and Rogiet railway sidings in the attic.

J23A   J23

Magor

The Gwent Federation of Women's Institutes produced a fine book on their villages, and documented Johnny Oily's travelling van, based in Magor, that, in the 1950s, supplied provisions to households in the area – everything from chocolate to paraffin.

More formal historical investigations have been carried out by the Monmouthshire Antiquarian Association regarding the impressive remnants of the Procurator's House, next to the church, dating from the sixteenth century and home of the vicar, appointed by the abbot of Tintern. It's the only one of its kind in Wales.

Caldicott

An excellent illustrated map explains lots of things about the town, including the state of play in 1086 when the Domesday Book recorded there were 15 half-villagers, 4 slaves and one man-at-arms at the command of the Lord of the Manor. Between them they possessed 12 ploughs and a mill, all of which was worth £6.

Now Caldicott has an early generation shopping mall that is refreshingly free of typical English mall chain stores. And the Castle offers evening entertainments that includes "Who killed the baron?" and "Who murdered Peggy Sue?"

STANDING STONE, ROGIET

(W.O.)
And now something just for the lorry drivers. Defying our own rules about sights being visible to car passengers, we thought this deserved to be an exception. The route of the motorway was re-positioned to allow this ancient stone to remain undisturbed. Who said those planners were uncaring? It's too close to the carriageway to be visible from a saloon car, but can be seen from the raised cab of your average 44 tonner travelling westward.

NEWPORT-GLOUCESTER/ BRISTOL

This is the main Swansea to Paddington line regularly monitored by train spotters. More than half the trains heading east are about to go into the Severn Tunnel, the rest will swing up the side of the Severn estuary towards Gloucester. Prior to the tunnel, the Bristol and South Wales Union Railway ran a service that took passengers to a dedicated terminal pier at Portskewett for a ferry across the estuary to meet the matching train on the other side.

And prior to that, another estuary ferry service offered to transport a coach and six horses from one side to the other for a few shillings.

HERITAGE BRICK WORKS (E.O.)
Edenhall cast stone products are made here from limestone and sandstone aggregates.

BARRIER SERVICES
Through the trees we can see the compound for this firm who carry out Highways Agency contracts for erecting or renewing barriers along motorways. It takes about 10 days to do a mile of central reservation barrier from scratch.

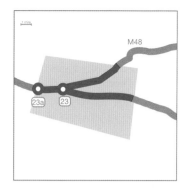

3060

M48 CONTINUES ON PAGE 88

IFTON INDUSTRIAL ESTATE
In the brown shed with the red ends is Royston Edwards's motorbike business. "A mad bugger", according to his partner Lisa, Royston was 6th in the Isle of Man 1987 race, and has recently changed to quad bike endurance racing.

CHERRY TREE CARE HOME (E.O.)
24-hour nursing and residential care. One of a dozen homes operated by Hallmark Healthcare, mostly in south and north Wales.

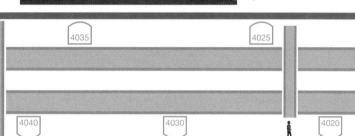

CALDICOT-CRICK
This disused line used to carry military materials to and from the Caerwent Munitions Factory that produced propellant for the Royal Navy in WW2. Crick is an enormous complex several square miles in size, still cordoned off by the MoD and used occasionally for training exercises. The Association of Industrial Archaeology notes that "secrecy prevails and little detail is known."

4035   4025

4040   4030   4020

TOLLS
Prices in 2005: Car £4.80; small goods vehicle £9.60; heavy goods vehicle and buses £14.30. But you don't pay at all if you only ever travel from west to east.

If three cars are passing through each minute during the day, that would amount to £3.8 million per annum.

Regular users are encouraged to invest in tags, an electronic device fitted to your car or lorry to automatically open a barrier "providing your account is in credit." And remember: "Offensive behaviour towards toll staff will lead to prosecution."

Spare a thought for Mr Wilmot, of Ifton Court, who suffered the daily blasts from the quarry next door that provided most of the hardcore for the base of this stretch of carriageway.

Monmouthshire
Often described as the least Welsh county in Wales, covering Chepstow, Usk and Abergavenny. One tourist information brochure promotes its pleasures in disguise referring simply to "Wye Valley and Vale of Usk". In exquisite Sunday colour magazine fashion, "an industrial archaeologist's paradise" is seamlessly blended with "tandem paragliding". Pointing out that the Wye tour has enthralled discerning visitors since the 18th century, they claim it's the "birthplace of British tourism."
ENGLISH-WELSH TRANSLATIONS ON PAGE 87.

Welcome to Wales
In March 2005, the London Observer newspaper devoted a page to Welsh Resurgence. Very timely as it was just one week before the rugby team won the Grand Slam.

Stimulus for the article was the forthcoming launch of the new wave Dr. Who TV show, made in Wales. Photo opportunity: Charlotte Church with her arm round a Dalek.

More than a third of Welsh children speak the language. If you don't know it, you can start to learn it by examining the translations of the road signs.

We anguished over replicating the Welsh translations on road signs in our entries, and, for reasons of space, eventually decided instead to devote a single page to covering all the translations, as well as some pronunciations and explanations, for which we are most grateful to Ian Davies and his colleagues at the Museum of Welsh Life.

The Welsh Books Council has plenty of accessible beginner texts.

Visit www.gwales.com for starters.

`38`

SEVERN RAILWAY TUNNEL

Audacious measures were pursued in the latter part of the 19th century to shorten the rail route to Wales from Bristol. Attempts to tunnel under the estuary ran into formidable problems, with water breaching the walls on a succession of occasions. A railway bridge at Sharpness opened in 1879. The owners offered its services to GWR who were funding the tunnel. Thomas Walker's diary documented the troubles below ground: "The water broke in from the bottom of the face of the heading, rolling up all at once like a great horse. It swept the men and the iron skips like so many chips." Deploying 36,000 tons of Portland cement and 76 million bricks, the tunnel eventually opened on 1st July 1887.

LINPAC METAL PACKAGING

You know that lovely old biscuit tin that your Grannie keeps things in – well, it might have come from here. They do all sorts of boxes made from metal, and back in WW2, these were mostly to keep ammunition in. These days the firm prefers to platform its capacity to create plastic containers.

ST REGIS PAPER MILL

Logs go in one end and corrugated card comes out the other. The plant can take tree trunks 3 metres long and 2/3rds of a metre diameter. These are churned into chips, then broken down into fibres which are combined with waste cardboard delivered by Severnside. The resulting pulp then enters the Benjamin paper machine that annually produces 145,000 tonnes of "semi-chemical" fluting – the corrugated card that forms the centre part between the outer layers of cardboard. The process uses 14 million litres of water a day which comes from the spring that plagued the railway tunnelers.

SUDBROOK PUMPING STATION

The rectangular building originally housed six Cornish beam engines powered by steam. They could shift 11,000 gallons a minute during the most difficult periods of the cutting of the railway tunnel under the estuary. On one day 30 million gallons were pumped out of the excavation. Now electric pumps keep the water levels in check, and only have to work hard when the Severn floods at spring tides. The building to the right is the original pump house.

SECOND SEVERN CROSSING

To ease pressure on the First Severn Bridge, this was constructed between 1992 and 1996. The overall length of the crossing is 5 kilometres and the main span, between the two 137 metre high towers, is 456 metres, and it sits 37 metres above high tide. Computer controlled barges accurately positioned cranes in the estuary to allow the establishment of the foundation caissons. 1,000 men were employed in the project that utilised 30,000 tons of steel and 300,000 cubic metres of concrete. The deck consists of 2,300 precast concrete segments each weighing 200 tonnes.

This magnificent crossing was opened by the Prince of Wales on 5th June 1996. (Picture: Page 89).

SEVERN ESTUARY

This is a dangerous place to go boating. The tidal range is 14 metres and the current can reach up to 9 knots.

Back in 1606 a combination of high tides and heavy rain caused the Severn to flood over an area 24 miles long by 4 miles wide, killing around 2,000 people and many more thousands of animals.

In 1926 an enterprising marine engineer established a ferry crossing that could deal with motorbikes as well as foot passengers. He'd handled ammunition train ferries across rivers in France during WW1, and was soon winching cars on and off his boat.

He built up a fleet of car ferries that allowed motorists to trim 55 miles off the journey from Bristol to Newport – subject to the weather, of course, which, in the winter of 1962/63 meant ice. Yes, part of the estuary froze over.

We got a shot of the Monika Muller.

FIRST SEVERN BRIDGE SEE PAGE 89

SOUTH WORTHY FARM

Derek Wookey was lambing when we called. 180 ewes were delivering about 320 lambs, half of which have to be helped out. The family are then penned because the ewe relies on smell to get to know her young. The lambs can stand and suckle after 15 minutes. After 16 weeks, they are ready for slaughter. The Severn once flooded to Derek's waist height and drowned the whole herd.

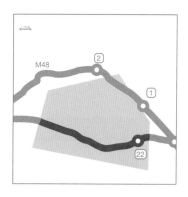

OLD SPLOTT RHINE

The network of drains here don't function like they used to. Mrs Hicks reckons the motorway contractors didn't adequately set pipework into the base of the carriageway, and that's why her land to the north of the carriageway is now always too wet, whilst the land to the south is too dry. Bath University's dense 'Economic Consequences of the Severn Bridge and its Associated Motorways' make no mention of this.

TAKING THEIR TOLL

The Second Severn Crossing takes about 75% of the daily bridge traffic of 35,000 vehicles. The first Severn Bridge was declared a Grade I listed building in 1998, with the adjoining stylish Wye Bridge (which lies over the English-Welsh border) a Grade II. The old bridge has to be painted every 5 years, which requires 250,000 litres of paint.

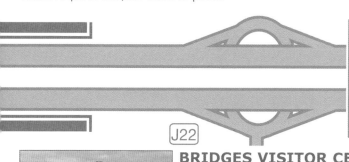

J22   3945   3930

BRIDGES VISITOR CENTRE (W.O.)

Get a sense of the extraordinary civil engineering achievement that lies to your west. A small independent charity that deserves better support and a bigger profile. Open 11 til 4 weekends and Bank Holidays, Easter to October.

TERRA WORKS

Liquid ammonium nitrate is sprayed from the top of this concrete tower. It turns into pellets of farmers' fertiliser as it falls. Behind the plant we can see the giant Transco storage tanks, holding household gas as a very cold liquid.

Avonmouth

One of Britain's most important ports. From here the structures look small, but when you drive into the complex the enormity of the cranes, compounds, warehouses and storage tanks is staggering. And some of the ships are colossal, dwarfing many of the harbourside buildings. Cars, chemicals, coal, timber, oil and food products account for much of the trade.

WALNING FARM

The Hicks changed to beef production after the motorway arrived because the dairy herd would not cross the bridge into the fields to the north. Mr Hicks and his son operate agricultural machinery leaving Mrs Hicks to mind 320 animals during the day. She knows them all personally and is saddened when they go to Baker's abattoir in Nailsea. Her husband takes ten in his wagon at seven in the morning so they don't have to queue. The meat is hung for 20 days and "melts in the mouth." She explained to us vegetarians that she doesn't connect a certain animal with her steak.

SEABANK

A state-of-the-art power station serving the whole of Bristol, driven by natural gas from the Transco plants. The exhaust is pumped to secondary recovery turbines making the plant much more efficient than conventional power stations.

OLVESTON

We can see the outskirts of this village which, unlike many of its neighbours, works hard to sustain some retail life at its heart – a village store and a newsagents. Let's hope they stay in business.

M48 CONTINUES ON PAGE 89

MEAD FARM

Jack Allen and son run their suckling cows business here. They had 7.9 acres but lost 1.5 acres to the new M4 route. Compensation was £3,000 an acre, but they would have preferred to keep the land.

FERNHILL COURT
(E.O.)

A complex of offices created by D20 who are also based here. They do ground work and civil engineering, that includes PFI school re-building in Bristol and Exeter, and re-directing a river so Asda could set up its Frome superstore. Behind the Court is Woodhouse Manor, also now serving as office accommodation.

HORTHAM HOSPITAL (W.O.)

When we came here three years ago we discovered a scrappy old site awaiting redevelopment. So imagine our surprise when we returned. It hasn't changed, but has a better fence round it, though not without gaps. Some day, we are assured, this will be a housing estate. It was a mental hospital from 1932 until 1994.

3879

J21   3889   J20

Wye Valley

The Wye springs to life close to the source of the Severn in north Wales, but the two rivers then go their separate ways before meeting again at Chepstow. The Wye meanders through the Forest of Dean and past Tintern Abbey on the way.
Best bit is Symonds Yat, of which the best bit for big kids is the Hedge Puzzle and Museum of Mazes. And make your way to the RSPB peregrine falcon viewing platform nearby.

Forest Of Dean

Which writers were inspired by this place? Pepys, Wordsworth, Tolkien, Dennis Potter and J.K. Rowling, according to the Dean Heritage Museum. So, get in those woods, then knock out a novel, TV play, diary or rhyme.

Tintern Abbey

"Stand amazed at the grandeur of Tintern Abbey, late in the day, after the crowds have gone," recommends the Wye Valley tourist guide. But what if everyone tries to follow this advice?

ST MARY THE VIRGIN, ALMONDS-BURY (E.O.)

There's a bit of a bend in the steeple, but it's stable and safe. Vicar Philip Rowe aims to offer you a genuine non-pressurised welcome; to accept you as you are – beliefs, disbeliefs, doubts and all.

M5

This runs from West Bromwich to Exeter. We drove along parts of it for many years before hitting on the idea of making a book out of the sights visible from the carriageway.

Were we mad, eccentric, obsessed, anorakish? No, it was a pleasure from start to finish. Fascinating to undertake the basic journalism of tracking down each structure then finding out what went on there.

The clever bit was finding a way of representing the information on consecutive pages. And that took a long time to figure out.

So can we summarise our first book here? Not really. We produced and sold 6,000 copies, and have no plans to update it. If you have a copy that you're finished with, please post it to the Oxfam Bookshop, 101 High Street, Worcester WR1 2HW. They are kindly acting as a clearing house for second hand copies. If you want to buy one, phone them on 01905 26967 or e-mail them on: shopf2228@oxfam.org.uk

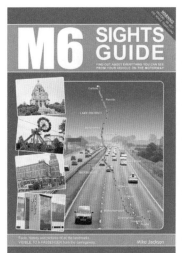

M6 SIGHTS GUIDE
FIND OUT ABOUT EVERYTHING YOU CAN SEE FROM YOUR VEHICLE ON THE MOTORWAY

Facts, history and pictures of all the landmarks VISIBLE TO A PASSENGER from the carriageway

Mike Jackson

HEADING NORTH?

Once you get to the top end of the M5, you will want a copy of this companion publication that covers everything along the 234 miles of the M6, from the M1 in Leicestershire up to the Lake District. Find out exactly where you pass over what's left of Hadrian's Wall east of Carlisle, and discover the source of the steam factory.

The New Statesman review explained that "Motorway scenery is a case study in the uneven development of capitalism, post-industrial detritus competing with swiftly assembled sheds to serve our mobile, just-in-time society." You can order The M6 Sights Guide from any good bookshop, or get it directly from severnpix (details on page 96).

THOSE ROVER MILES

We used to commute to Bristol from Worcester up and down the M5 in our old Rover 214, and then we researched our M5 Sights Guide in it, taking the mileage up to 140,000. We again most gratefully acknowledge MG Rover's support with this book which has allowed us to cruise along in a fine 45 Club SE.

ALMONDSBURY JUNCTION

The M5 and the M4 meet here in the midst of a four-layer structure that in total consists of 7 miles of roadway. It was opened by the Queen in September 1966, thus connecting the M4 and the Filton bypass with south Wales across the first Severn Bridge. The M5 got here from Gloucester in 1971.

ALMONDSBURY

This village got off relatively unscathed with the routing of both the M4 and M5 on the ridges to its east. But the value of land was transformed by its newly acquired accessibility to all parts. Some allotments, priced at £1,000 in 1946, were put on the market in 1988 and fetched over £3 million. The Parish Council has since been plagued by battles over the deployment of the cash.

NHS DIRECT (W.O.)

In here dozens of nurses tell you what to do when you're not well.

The building also houses the Avon Ambulance Service Emergency Dispatch Centre handling 100,000 calls a year.

ORANGE (E.O.)

How many masts serve the M4? We used our mobile to ring Customer Services who told us the Press Office was not a "customer-facing" number.

We tracked down their Media Centre which has an answerphone saying "leave a message and we'll get back to you". We did, and they didn't. Too busy churning out 80 page magazines celebrating their successes.

APEX COURT

Twin roof turrets demark blocks 8 and 9 of the 20-odd office buildings in Apex Court. Amongst the tenants are builders Henry Boot, The Gaming Board for Great Britain (South West region), the Office for Standards in Education and the Society for Endocrinology.

GREENCORE

If you've ever bought a chilled tub of pasta sauce in a supermarket, chances are it came from here. What used to be the Irish Sugar Corporation now supply supermarkets with sauces and soups in plastic pots, of which they fill 30 million in a year, getting through 3,000 tons of tomatoes in the process.

TRAVEL THROUGH TIME

One hundred years ago most of us worked in the one place all of our lives, and hardly ever went anywhere else. Now we roar down motorways, directed by satellite navigation whilst talking on hands-free mobile phones. What will we be up to in another 100 years?

RAC TOWER

As this is the key sight that appears in both the M5 and M4 Sights Guides, we thought we'd better dig out some fresh information on it for our loyal readership, so we Googled the name and location and discovered that one of the Google entries is the Index to our M5 book. Em, it was designed by Nicholas Grimshaw and opened in 1995.

Aviva has recently bought the RAC and stuck it in bed with the Norwich Union, shedding many jobs here in the process.

ST MICHAEL THE ARCHANGEL, WINTERBOURNE

Associated with the Bradeston family from the 14th century. Thomas Bradeston was close to the Berkeleys, and, following the murder of Edward II, gained a knighthood and this Manor. "At Court he is like a little saint, in his county like a raging lion." The church was in the Diocese of Worcester until 1542 when a Bishopric of Bristol was created by Henry VIII.

Bristol

Impossible to convey the rich diversity and charm of this great city briefly. A vibrant and engaging place that benefits greatly from its harbour frontages. Bristol has always been big on transport and communication. Much of the wealth of Bristol was generated in the 17th century by shipping merchants, and then Bristolians had Brunel pop into town to lay down a few railway lines and advance the principles of steam. Lots of pioneering aircraft design and subsequent successful production has emerged from the area, not least through British Aerospace and Rolls Royce. The BBC's Natural History Unit and Antiques Roadshow productions are based here, but of course require considerable travelling to distant parts to gather the necessary footage. It's also the home of Wallace and Gromit, the Creature Comforts and other delightful and distinctive stop-frame animation creations from Nick Park and Aardmann. And Bristol's big on balloons. Our most vivid memory is directing a dawn concert for Music Live with ten Cameron hot air balloons doing flame effects in the background. We think the city should take on responsibility for the admirable but under-supported Severn Bridge Visitors' Centre, to complete a portfolio of transport triumphs.

WINTERBOURNE

This was a big centre for felt hat-making in the 17th century. Raw materials came from local rabbits mixed with beaver fur shipped in from Canada. And the market for the end product? Slaves on sugar plantations in the West Indies who worked better if provided with protection from the sun and the rain.

GLOUCESTER/SWINDON–PARKWAY

Constructed in 1905 to take advantage of the Severn tunnel and to by-pass Bath, to establish a fast route from Cardiff to London. At Yate to the north east it splits to Gloucester and Swindon; beyond Parkway it divides three ways towards Wales, Avonmouth and Bristol Temple Meads.

AMCOR

As you know, most stuff in medical centres comes wrapped in plastic. Well, a lot of that plastic comes from here. It's a Cast Films Centre of Excellence creating sophisticated rollstock to pack drugs and medical devices.
A new business park is being developed behind, next to the motorcycle training centre.

BRISTOL BUSINESS PARK

Building 240 offers 18,000 square feet at £21.50 per square foot per annum, and 88 car park spaces on "Bristol's exclusive office campus."

WAVERLEY COTTAGE

In the outbuilding is Initially Yours, embroiderers who do personalised logos on workwear, schoolwear and sportswear. "You name it, we stitch it".

Parkway

A useful connection point for travellers to and from the north (Birmingham and beyond) and south west (Devon and Cornwall) to pick up or leave trains travelling east west. Paddington to Swansea takes less than 3 hours.

ROBERTS BROS.

They have been plantsmen since 1830, supplying Bristol market with lettuce, red cabbage, parsley and beetroot. When the supermarkets eliminated many greengrocers, they started to specialise in hanging baskets containing a range of 20 plants.

VILLAGE HOSPITAL
(E.O.)
This was a state of the art facility in 1905, sitting in Hambrook, which was hacked in half by the route of the M4, and further suffered from being the northern end of the M32 link motorway into the centre of Bristol.

THE WHITE HORSE (E.O.)
Les Brooker has been landlord for 27 years, and puts up with the ghost in the beer cellar that turns on taps in the night. He's had several lorries crash into the beer garden after they've lost control on Whiteshill.

Proud of the food and his catering for children, Les fears the ban on smoking will kill the pub trade.

MOOREND FARM
Garth O'Donnell got this property relatively cheap following an auction in which it didn't reach its reserve. He raised the cash with friends and they've now split it into three separate dwellings, being tastefully restored.

The building dates from 1676 and boasted an exterior five-seater privy, divided into segments for family and farm worker use.

The house was at one time owned by Richard Champion, a pioneer of porcelain in the Bristol area.

CHANGING BEHAVIOUR
Alastair Darling has recently opened up discussions on applying journey-based pricing to our motoring. Fair chance Bristol is in his sights as somewhere to pilot schemes. It's got good bus services, but limited rail offerings due to the steep hills up from the River Avon. Of course, at some point in the future, anxieties about the impact of the internal combustion engine may become academic, because the world is running out of oil. Could these carriageways eventually be deserted? Watch this space.

RIVER FROME
This springs around Yate and feeds Bristol harbour. The Environment Agency recently published a Consultation Document on the Bristol Avon Catchment Abstraction Management Strategy which determined that there was sufficient water available in here to continue issuing licences for drawing out water for household, industrial or agricultural use.

BRISTOL AIRPORT
In 2001 they handled 2.8 million passengers; by 2003 the figure was 3.8. Projections suggest the figure could reach 12 million by 2030. Em, great for the local economy and all those fortunate holiday makers, but what is this amount of flying doing to the globe? Every aircraft flight contributes detrimentally to climate change. Stay at home and save the planet.

RING ROAD
Bristol is coming close to setting up congestion charging. Parts of the ring road are allocated to multi-occupied vehicles, i.e. a driver on his or her own can't use certain lanes. During morning peak the queue of vehicles trying to get on the ring road can extend several miles either side of the M32.

Kingswood
The rise and fall of local cottage industries is well documented in the Kingswood History Project booklets. Before the introduction of machinery in the 1830s, pin-making at home from factory-produced wire was a vital occupation. This was replaced by boot manufacture led by Fussell and Flook who introduced riveting for sole attachment to this industrious community.

FRENCHAY HOSPITAL
Spare a thought for visitors not on the route of public transport. Between 2 and 4 hours in the car park costs £3.20. And that applies every day and night of the year. There's talk of the place being downgraded to a cottage hospital.

M32 CONTINUES ON PAGES 90 AND 91

3785

3770

ACR

They operate a Resource Recycling Unit for Sainsburys, washing and returning half a million plastic crates to suppliers each week, and sending 2,000 bales of cardboard from stores to a Kent papermill.

MOT MANAGEMENT

The Department of Transport Vehicle and Operator Services Agency is based in Bristol. They are paying Siemens £250 million to monitor, manage and improve the efficiency of Britain's 19,000 MOT Test centres, 17,000 Authorised Examiners and 55,000 MOT testers.

SAINSBURY'S DISTRIBUTION CENTRE

Over 800 people work here across 40,000 square metres of floor space, preparing lorry loads for 50 stores in the south west – from Hereford to Swansea, from Newbury to Truro, with logistical help from Exel.

See Felicity Lawrence's 'Not on the Label' and Joanna Blythman's 'Shopped' for the behind the scenes on supermarkets.

VIVA

Bristol is home to the biggest campaigning vegetarian organisation in the world set up ten years ago by Juliet Gellatley. VIVA mount audacious media campaigns and directly confront organisations guilty of animal abuse. Paul McCartney, Martin Shaw, Jenny Seagrove and Joanna Lumley are amongst their celebrity supporters. There are over 5 million vegetarians in the UK, nearly one in ten of the population.

WHITE CAT STABLES (W.O.)

The long low building is the indoor training arena for this security conscious equestrian centre. Behind it are the Howsmoor boarding kennels at Whitehouse Farm, and to the west are a pair of local radio masts.

MURCO OIL TERMINAL

Rail wagons bring petrol, diesel and kerosene from the refinery at Milford Haven to this place. It's pumped into tanks and then loaded into road wagons for delivery to retail, commercial and domestic customers.

The terminal was set up in 1990. Each rail wagon has a payload of 70 tonnes which constitutes about 90,000 litres of petrol.

LEIGH FARM (W.O.)

Water supply has been a problem since the motorway cut the farm in two, because the 2 inch pipe under the carriageway became clogged with concrete and a 1 inch pipe was run through it. Mr Humphreys created some woodland on the site of construction spoil that is now home to a badger set.

When one of his cows escaped on to the carriageway, lots of people phoned the police, who thought a whole herd were loose. The animal crossed all six lanes, but Mr Humphries managed to get her back home safely.

WESTERFIELD CREMATORIUM

This was farm land until 1972. The farmer's neighbours didn't want the development, but the farmer was glad to sell the land so they didn't formally object. Normal planning permission does not have to be pursued in order for a council to set up a crematorium. It offers a "modern and rural alternative to people in the Bristol and Bath area." Down the road is a pet cemetery, doubtless equally capable of generating strong emotion.

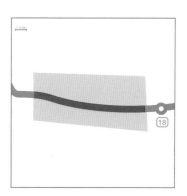

BARLEYCLOSE FARM, CODRINGTON

On the western edge of what was the Dodington estate, that was once occupied by Sir Edward Codrington, who had charge of the Orion at Trafalgar, and later commanded the Allied Fleets of England, France and Russia at the Battle of Navarino.

PARKFIELD COALMINE (E.O.)

Regular seams, free of faults made this area a thriving coal resource, employing 10 year olds and upwards. The mine was shut in 1936, having become uneconomic following the opening of the Severn tunnel which allowed Bristol to get cheap coal from south Wales. The chimney is all that remains on the surface. (The chimney further south marks the site of Shortwood brickworks.)

THOMAS A BECKET, PUCKLECHURCH

The Saxon king Edmund the Grand was stabbed to death by an outlaw near here. These days a group of parents are working hard to provide activities for young people hanging round the streets who "occasionally upset village residents and in some cases understandably so." Trouble-free is the delightful Coach House café.

BARLEYCLOSE FARM, PUCKLECHURCH

Alvin Taylor is glad to have the M4 close by because it allows him to transport 15 tonne loads of hay for stables eastward and fodder for cattle westward.

Following a shop robbery in Chippenham, the police pursued a man in a car to this point on the carriageway. He climbed into Alvin's field and hid in the runner beans. Police surrounded the field and got Alvin to take them on the back of his tractor through the crops until they tracked the fugitive down.

HINTON

The green sheds mark the edge of this village once dominated by the Grange which is now a Hotel, described in the Johannesen Book as "a hopelessly romantic if somewhat slightly eccentric retreat." Behind the hill is Dyrham Park, dating from 1692, now in the hands of the National Trust and achieving four stars in Simon Jenkins's 'England's Thousand Best Houses': "still as William Blathwayt built it, the east façade is a superbly romantic composition."

ST MARY MAGDALENE, TORMARTON (W.O.)

A plaque inside declares that in 1842 Mrs Sarah Manning, widow, gave to the Trustees £366.12s.1d "to lay out Dividends arising therefrom in Bread, and distribute the same on 22nd February every year amongst the Poor Male and Female Inhabitants of the Parish, as should not at the time be inmates of the Workhouse, in such proportions as the Trustees should think fit and proper."

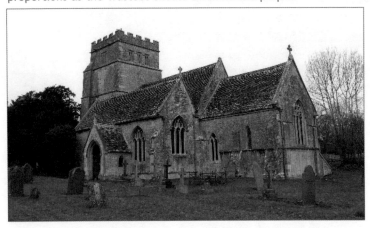

COTSWOLD WAY

This 102 mile footpath runs from Chipping Campden to Bath and crosses the M4 here, about 100 miles from both ends of the motorway, and where we briefly pass through the southern peninsula of the Cotswold Area of Outstanding Natural Beauty.

Stroud

We once scrounged a ride in a glider to get some 'helicopter' shots of a wind turbine. The pilot was determined we would get good angles of the structure and so threw us around the skies for 10 minutes or more. It was a horrible experience, bringing us out in a sweat in the cramped cockpit and leaving us feeling ill for hours once mercifully back on the ground.

BARRY'S STEEL SHED (E.O.)

Okay, it's not the greatest sight, but behind it lies the village of Acton Turville, which has much to commend it, not least Nicki Harrington, the daughter of one of the landladies of the Fox and Hounds, who told us this was where James Dyson lived when he invented the ball barrow. The Buffer Depot at the old railway station was an MoD field ration store. And in a 1981 snowstorm the Queen became stranded and took refuge in a nearby hotel.

3637

J18

3652

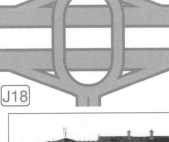

LOWER LAPDOWN FARM

Robin Berry is a cheerful man who doesn't have a problem with the motorway. His parents' land was hardly affected by the route of the carriageway, and as a youngster he enjoyed watching the construction process. He's had far more problems with the routing of the Cotswold Way across his fields. He's discovered litter on the pathway, and has seen motorcyclists heading along it, much to the consternation of horse riders. And one of his wooden gates was stolen, probably for firewood.

WESTFIELD FARM

Now a private home, this was the Daniels' Farm Museum. The couple took the place on in 1966 as a dairy, corn and potatoes business, but became frustrated with the economics and so set up a farm museum in 1988. They closed that in 1999, and now run a gardening business, looking after the homes of the growing numbers of incoming yuppies too busy to tend to their plants, which Mr Daniels greatly enjoys.▼

REWARDS FOR INFORMATION

In the 1830s the Castle Coombe Association published a tariff of rewards for information on Oath on Persons guilty of offences: Murder, burglary housebreaking, Highway Robbery or setting Fire to Dwelling House, Barn or other outbuilding £5. 5s 0d. Stealing any waggons, cart, plough or other implement of husbandry £2.2s.0d.

Bath

Margaret Baker wrote a fact-packed pocket guide to the Bath mail-coach Road, published by Shire of Tring in 1968, and dedicated to John Palmer of Bath, 1742-1818, creator of the mail coach service. Bizarre Bath is an evening comic guided walk, and a cheap and easy way of doing what we tried in Birmingham with our 'Spaghetti Junction' theatre restaurant shows.

ALL SAINTS, LITTLETON DREW

Pevsner didn't dwell on this place: "Thin perp central tower. Otherwise by T.H. Wyatt 1856. Or is the Perp w window original?" On our visit we discovered that the oldest of its three bells came from Bristol Foundry in 1480.

Wiltshire

So much to say, so little space. As the Tourist Guide points out: 'Wise travellers know that the slower you go, the more you see'. The County has a 168 mile cycleway that links some of the 100 plus locations where you can buy locally grown food (see the Harvest directory). And they are encouraging Walking Buses whereby supervised kids crocodile to school instead of being ferried by car or fancy four-wheeler.

Westonbirt

You're a big cheese in Wiltshire Victorian society. How do you impress your rich friends? By sticking exotic trees right across your estate; why even moving the village and the road to improve the landscaping prospects. That's what Robert Holford did, but 100 years later you couldn't see the wood for the trees, so the whole caboodle became a branch of the Forestry Commission, who made it the National Arboretum, logging every one of the 18,000 specimens in 600 acres, down the road from Highgrove where the heir to the throne resides with his new wife.

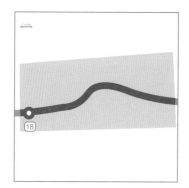

AUTHORISED VEHICLES

There's a padlocked gate at the bottom of this access track. It sits on the Fosse Way, the Roman road that runs in a straight line from Bath, through Cirencester to Leicester. Just south of here in the 1960s a Roman temple to the God Apollo was excavated, and the Wiltshire and Swindon Biological Records Centre are currently accumulating wildlife data.

ST MARY THE VIRGIN, BURTON

The building dates from 1290 and belonged to Glastonbury Abbey until the Dissolution. It now lies within the Diocese of Bristol, which in 2004 requested a payment of £4,086 from the parish towards meeting its diocesan costs.

Down the road is Hillside Garage. On the side of their recovery truck they say: "We met by accident".

PUMPING STATION

Transco's Littleton Drew site moves unodorised natural gas underground. Drew is thought to be a reference to Druids. Just south of here are the remains of an ancient tumulus 60 metres by 30 metres.

COACH STYLE

The big green shed is the headquarters of a firm that operates a dozen coaches available for private hire or organised tours. It's in the hamlet of Gibb (from gibbet?) where they cut down their hanging tree in 1941.

WEST FOSCOTE HOUSE

As with Sevington School, we nipped round the far side so you could see another exquisite example of the Neeld building investments. Keith Melhuish's study describes it as "part picturesque folly and part farmhouse", the central square bell tower surmounted by a ribbed, copper dome and weathercock.

Castle Combe Circuit

An enormous heart-shaped track surrounded by a bank to deaden the noise and lessen the likelihood of a competitor flying off into the trees. If you are less that 6 feet 8 inches tall and weigh under 20 stone, you can have a go at driving a racing car. Drivers must complete an indemnity form upon arrival. Down the road is 1962's prettiest village in England, which got it the role of a seaside town in 'Doctor Dolittle'.

GRITTLETON

A few buildings in the village are visible, though not Grittleton House which is now a posh private school ('To strive is to accomplish'; Juniors £1,716.00 per term). It was the home of Joseph Neeld, who got rich quick and married Lady Caroline Ashley-Cooper, daughter of the Earl of Shaftsbury, on New Year's Day 1831. But four days later they were separated, and a long, complicated court case followed wherein he was alleged to be keeping an illegitimate daughter in the village and Lady Caroline was described as having "mercenary motives".

After that Neeld concentrated on commissioning architect James Thomson to do up various properties in the area.

ST MARGARET OF ANTIOCH

Joseph Neeld (1789-1856) is buried here. He worked for his uncle, a London jeweller, and looked after the old man for the last 14 years of his life, which led to Neeld inheriting a fortune in 1827. Neeld became M.P. for Chippenham on the proceeds and bought the Grittleton estate which included Leigh Delamere. "He loved to pass his days to use well the talents entrusted to his stewardship."

LEIGH DELAMERE SERVICES EASTBOUND

This is one of only two service areas that operates a Barber's Shop. It's been going for two years, and was recently taken over by William Barton from Trowbridge. 40% of his customers are lorry drivers, many of whom get a shave as well. He was cutting one man's hair and recognised the customer's voice but couldn't place it. William asked where he knew the voice from and Dan Maskell told him it was from tennis commentary. William would be rich if he got a pound for every time someone asks him where the cash point is.

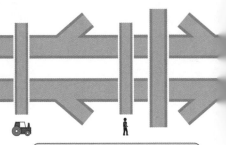

SEVINGTON SCHOOL

Built in 1848 from spare bits of Leigh Delamere church, including the 14th century bell tower, the school served village children until 1913. And since 1991 it has been a Victorian School again, thanks to some enterprising and talented teachers who run classes for visiting school parties, with everyone dressed in period costume - a delightful trip back in time of unique educational value.

LEIGH DELAMERE SERVICES WESTBOUND

Great place for celebrity spotting. The staff told us they'd seen Noel Gallagher, Michael Parkinson, Denise van Outen, Dawn French, Jennifer Saunders, Charlotte Church, Sharon Davies, Kylie Minogue, Bob Mortimer, Shane Richie, Hugh Grant, Simon Cowell, Johnny Wilkinson, Lawrence Delalio, Simon le Bon, Jim Davidson and Robbie Williams. Julie Attwood was serving in the shop when she was advised Lynford Christie was on his way. She said: "I'll be able to check out the size of his lunchbox", and turned round to discover Mr Christie was standing right by her at the till. He laughed.

YATTON KEYNELL WATER TOWER

This holds 1 million litres of water which is about 10 hours worth of peak demand for the surrounding villages. There's a ground tank alongside and water is constantly pumped up into the tower by Wessex Water.

Chippenham

Motor vehicle access through here is pinched by the proximity of the River Avon and the Brunel viaduct carrying the railway from Bath to Swindon. Goodness knows how problematic it was before the M4 came along to draw traffic off the A4. But persevere and you'll find a car park in order to explore the pedestrianised High Street (the old A4) and the very pleasing new Heritage Centre spread through the rooms of a Georgian building on the site of King Alfred's Hunting Lodge.

STANTON MANOR

The original building was once owned by the Chief Minister to Queen Elizabeth the First, William Cecil, Baron of Burghley (yes, think Stephen Fry in 'Blackadder II').

It's now a fine hotel and restaurant, where we could overhear frenetic participants on a training course hyping up about core drives, exploiting opportunities and developing skill sets to achieve blue chip methodology. They were from a High Street bank. Scary.

Cirencester

Most of what is the current Cotswold town was once a Roman settlement. You can't see any sign of its Roman roots on the streets, but below them there's plenty of evidence, the best of which has been dug up and is on display in a beautifully appointed museum.

In 1400, a group of frustrated noblemen took up arms against Henry VI and set fire to some houses in Cirencester to distract approaching Royal troops. The townsmen sought revenge, "wherein both the Duke of Surrey and Earl of Salisbury were slain; their heads were cut off, and sent to London." In return the King rewarded the locals with one Hogshead of wine "out of the Port of our Town of Bristol" every year "for the time being," according to Atkyns's 'State of Glostershire'.

Cirencester is a lovely place with old frontages determining the look of the streets. Park out of town and walk in. You'll be glad you came here.

CELEB SPOTTERS

should travel one mile north of Junction 17 to visit the 24-hour Murco/Costcutter frequented by Liz Hurley and Christine Hamilton.

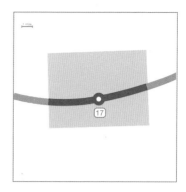

HUNGERDOWN HOUSE

Built in 1914, with gardens designed by Percy Cane, 1881-1976, publisher of My Garden Illustrated and Garden Design magazines.

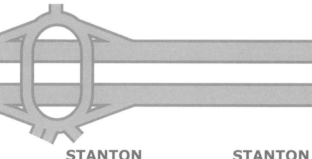

CUT BACKS

A farmer explained to us the economics of managing 200 sheep. It costs £300 to pay two shearers to work through the herd (one and a half minutes per animal). And the resulting wool fetches just £260, whereas 10 years ago, the Wool Board would have paid £500 for that quantity. A lamb is worth about £50, the same as 10 years ago. Problem is Brazilian sheep are much cheaper.

STANTON MAINTENANCE COMPOUND

This is a back-up gritter base run by WS Atkins. We asked them about Mr Millard's problems (Page 51) and they assured us they send out emergency crews if carriageway fencing is broken by a vehicle, because they don't want a cow getting on to the motorway. The orange netting is only used for a field of barley to keep rabbits in, not stock.

STANTON RECYCLING CENTRE

People bring 8,500 tonnes of rubbish here each year, three times as much in August as in January. The tall steel structure is the old compactor station, now disused, and the green arms are roll packers for crushing wood and cardboard into skips. Almost 70% of the household waste is recycled, but everything stops when they discover a tank shell in a skip. Then the site is isolated until the army come to remove it. The operators will also search the paper bank for your missing watch or engagement ring if you're nice to them.

ALL SAINTS, SUTTON BENGER

In the graveyard is a memorial to the 12 local men who gave their lives "for King and Country in the Great War", and one of them also gets a marble plaque inside: John Randolph Lea, 7th Gloucester Regiment, only son of John and Lucy Lea. Oct 6th 1915 aged 20 years. Buried in Chatby Cemetery, Alexandria.

Bowood House

Sitting on the A4 between Chippenham and Calne, the building only gets two stars in 'England's Thousand Best Houses', possibly because the 8th Marquess of Lansdowne demolished the 'Big' Bowood House in 1955, then cleared off to Scotland leaving the Earl of Shelburne with the "challenge" of occupying the 'Little' House and running a tourist attraction from it.

RIVER AVON

Okay, geographers, which way is it flowing? South. It starts life in Badminton Park to the west of here, then comes through Malmesbury before heading past this point to swing west towards Bideford-on-Avon and Bath before running through Bristol and out to the Severn estuary. Talking of Malmesbury, whilst it doesn't get a blue or brown destination sign, it's well worth a visit, for its neat artefacts museum, and the wonderful old garage premises, still selling second hand cars, halfway up the rather ordinary main street.

DODFORD COTTAGE

Lots of effective diversification on and around Dodford Farm, not least the Daycare Nursery occupying old farm buildings up the lane. Kim Branston supervises indoor and outdoor activities, including plenty of enjoyable farm walks, followed by a healthy two course cooked lunch. Collect your child in time to avoid the late pick up charges.

UNION FARM

This looks across to the tree-lined mile drive established to allow Lady Meux to make a quick dash to the railway station at Dauntsey in Victorian times. She was an actress, married to an Earl occupying Dauntsey Hall, for which this place was an estate farm. She kept a pet tiger that menaced the Rector, and paid for a stained glass image of her face to be inserted in the east window of St James the Great church.

BRINKWORTH EARL DANBY C.E. PRIMARY SCHOOL

This is the Dauntsey lower school site. Head Teacher Mrs Brierley is keen to encourage good parenting and operates 'Bridge the Gap' classes for Mums and Dads. She points out that "children, unlike mobile phones and DVD players, do not come with a handbook complete with tips for getting them going, maintaining them and dealing with problems."

3458

3429

3473

3444

DODFORD LANE POULTRY UNIT

An all day and night nursery for chickens.

THE CHIMNEY

This was a milk churn manufacturing unit in Dauntsey Lock. It's now home to a host of microbusinesses. The owner lives in a house called The Comedy, but he didn't seem to see the funny side of our book.

CLACK ABBEY

The 14th century tower is all that remains of an Augustinian Priory founded in 1142. It's on the brow of the hill in the village of Bradenstoke. There was more but it was removed in the 1930s by William Randolph Hearst to tart up his Welsh holiday home, St. Donat's Castle. The ghosts of a monk and a dog are said to haunt what's left.

RAF Lyneham

The aircraft circling south of the motorway are coming into this operational base, which hit the headlines on the day of the Iraq elections, Sunday 31st January 2005. A Hercules with 10 men aboard crashed on a flight north from Baghdad.

The bodies of the men were returned to Lyneham on Tuesday 8th February, to be met by their family, friends and colleagues, and the Princess Royal, honorary air commodore of the base, and the Defence Secretary Geoff Hoon.

We were touched by the many tributes at the gates, one of which read:

"With deepest sympathy and condolences, our Lyneham Heroes who have paid the ultimate price for Democracy and Peace in the World. An elite and so, so Special Team, with special thoughts, Andy Humm."

WATSON PETROLEUM

Tony Watson was based at RAF Lyneham at the end of WW2. He set up a small business here in Brinkworth to buy and sell fuel, and more than sixty years on is still at it with the help of his family. They provide homes, businesses and some petrol stations in the South West with all types of fuel. This is their Head Office up on the ridge above Dauntsey Vale.

ST MICHAEL & ALL ANGELS' CHURCH, BRINKWORTH

A fund-raising thermometer board shows red up to £20,000 as the first notch on a goal towards £150,000 needed for roof restoration. Down the road we found Mr Chesterman's motorcycle sales and service shop. Inside were lots of second-hand bicycles, two motor scooters (including a Triumph T10 at £100 "Cheap to clear") and a three-layer tea trolley ("half price £30").

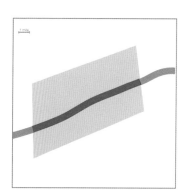

DOVEY'S FARM

Those outbuildings where Mrs Howell keeps her horses aren't so satisfactory when you get up close. Mr Howell said they are not DIY but Disaster Yourself, erected by the previous occupiers.

HOSTAGE SITUATION

It was here that the motor-caravan ran out of petrol. A distressed estranged father kidnapped his child, allegedly by gunpoint, and was pursued by the police along the motorway. The officers surrounded the vehicle and hovered helicopters overhead, hailing demands that the man hand over his child. The motorway was closed for four days, much to the delight of those living alongside.

3399

3414

LUKER'S FARM

The green sheds demark this stud for breeding and training dressage horses.

Mrs Wilkinson visited what had been a derelict turkey farm five times before she decided to buy it and turn it into an equestrian complex 9 years ago. She's planted 900 trees to screen the warm-blooded cross thoroughbreds from the motorway.

VINES FARM

Mr Millard is committed to his dairy farm despite its difficulties and limited rewards. He was furious about the way the original contractors ran roughshod over his land as soon as the compulsory purchase orders had been delivered. These days his biggest problem comes from cars crashing through the fences and the poor efforts of the Highways Agency contractors to mend those fences. They temporarily use plastic screens which they claim are stock-proof, but the cows push them down. One workman told him that he was covered, insurance-wise, if a cow caused a multiple pile-up. Mr Millard felt that was hardly the point.

HOOKER'S GATE FARM

John Brice's 70-strong dairy herd is organic, the milk going to Yeo Valley Yoghurts. Organic cows graze on pastures free of artificial insecticides, herbicides or fungicides. Hedges and meadows are seldom disturbed so wildlife can flourish.

But very disturbing are the cars that skew off the motorway and career into the fields. It's an accident blackspot. One car recently killed a cow.

WHO'D BE A FARMER?

You're responsible for the stewardship of a vast tract of land. You need lots of expensive machines to manage those fields. Animals require constant attention. And you can't plan your time as everything's so weather dependent.

We want our countryside to be in good order, but have little sense of the dedication of relatively few people to sustaining this challenging but vital way of life.

BEWARE OF ATTACK WIFE

That's what the sign on the gate says at a house just up the road from here. Is this funny, a peculiar expression of sexism, disrespect for women, male masochism, a warning of female proprietorial tendencies or what? Short answers on a postcard, please.

HOOK W.I.

The ladies occupy the village hall every second Tuesday in the month for various events including competing over: best Winter photograph, small piece of needlework, greeting card, vase of spring flowers, knitted bootees, unusual cheese recipe and Christmas Floral Basket (arranged on the night).

SCHOOL HOUSE RESTAURANT (W.O.)

This was the school for the village of Hook, but it now houses a fancy restaurant. Starters start at £7.50 (for an olive and tomato salad with spring onions on shredded leaf lettuce with gooseberry dressing).

BRISTOL-SWINDON

This is the main line on which we can see 8-carriage First Great Western trains and 25-wagon English and Welsh Railway freight trains. The track swings south east from here to join the Bath line just south of Wootton Bassett before crossing under the motorway again to head into Swindon.

The ingenuity and energy of Brunel is in evidence along most of the M4, as it inevitably keeps passing stretches of what was the great engineer's track and accompanying support structures. And let's remember the men who did the hard labour. In those days there were no JCBs.

Cotswold Water Park

Sand and gravel has been extracted south east of Cirencester for 150 years to support civil engineering, first for railways, then roads, and it still goes on today. The 100 leftover lakes are being turned into an enormous inland leisure complex. Source of the Thames, there are dozens of water sports facilities, cycling prospects and nature reserves. Start at the Gateway Centre just off the A419. Great guides, café and fossils.

3383

3354

3369

ST BARTHOLOMEW AND ALL SAINTS, WOOTTON BASSETT

In the porch a sign reads: "Friend, you enter this church, not as a stranger but as a Guest of God. Be grateful for the strong and loyal men who in the name of Jesus Christ built this place of worship, and to all who have beautified it and hallowed it with their prayers and praises."

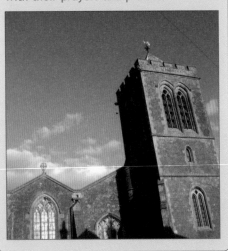

"OLDEST AND BEST"

Wiltshire was the first English county to have a police force, on duty since 1839.

WIND PUMP

Simple but effective technology. When the wind blows, the blades drive a two metre deep pump to push water to a tank at the top of the field for irrigating parts of Midge Hall Farm.

Wootton Bassett

This busy place has a museum in its old Town Hall, a 17th century black and white structure sitting atop stone stilts. Visit on Saturday mornings to find lovely artefacts, great photographs and enthusiastic volunteers (some full of praise for benefactor Lady Meux - more about her on Page 50).

They told us of how a German field gun was presented to the town in 1919 but local ex-servicemen decided they'd faced enough of such weapons, so they shoved it off its plinth one night and it rolled down the hill into a stream where it remained for many years until it was taken off for scrap to create munitions for World War Two (WW2).

These days they are big on recycling in Wootton Bassett and have advice on a future life for everything from CDs (bird-scarers) to ice cream tub spoons (spreading glue), from lolly sticks (plant labels) to toothbrushes (cleaning alloy wheels).

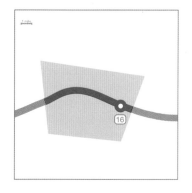

HOMEBASE REGIONAL DISTRIBUTION CENTRE

(E.O.)

The Lydiard Fields Depot can hold 26,000 pallets in its 356,500 square feet. They prepare 205 deliveries a week to 127 stores. Nationally, they have 300 stores and 1 million customers a week. Recently the Soil Association awarded them their first Chain of Custody certificate for ethical trading principles promoting good forest management to ensure its timber products come from legal and well managed sources.

BRUNEL TOWER (E.O.)

The tallest building in Swindon at 52 metres, in the heart of the shopping centre. It was opened in 1976 as the Murray John Building in honour of the Borough's Town Clerk who had held that role since 1938 until his death in 1974.

It's shared between private residents and office tenants. It's UK Head Office for Ecolab, global leaders in sanitising products for restaurants, hotels and hospitals.

JOHNSON MATTHEY FUEL CELLS (W.O.)

There are two cream-coloured big units adjacent to each other on the Lydiard Fields complex. Homebase, with a white top, is visible only whilst travelling eastward. This one, with a grey top, is where the multinational chemical company are developing the principles and practices of fuel cells. An electrochemical device reacts hydrogen and oxygen without burning to produce electricity cleanly and efficiently. Early days, and fingers crossed, however American environmental campaigner Ralph Nader reckons such things are just "razzle dazzle technological dreams", though a motorbike firm recently launched a prototype fuel-cell-powered machine that seemed to work but was disconcertingly quiet.

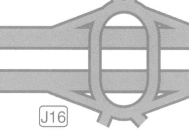

3339

J16

SPITTLEBOROUGH FARM

This house became a site office when the land on the other side of the carriageway was developed for business use. Property developers ICP Commercials have now made it their offices. They were responsible for the Johnson Matthey plant opposite, and continue to work on projects along the M4 corridor.

Swindon

There once was a tiny town called Swindon, then the Great Western Railway came along and needed a decent depot halfway between Reading and Bristol. The Borough housed what became one of the biggest railway works in the world, occupying 300 acres and employing 12,000 men before WW1, but things declined after WW2, and then Swindon became seen as a spot suitable for development as a new town.

WH Smith's headquarters has been here since 1967. They employ 1,000 people managing the logistics of over 500 High Street shops, from where you can buy our Motorway Sights Guides. Up the road at South Marston, Honda employ 4,000 people making the new Civic that will be exported to Japan.

Park and Ride Schemes allow you to watch the bus driver negotiate alarming but effective multi-roundabouts on the way.

Famous Swindonians? Diana Dors, born Diana Fluck in 1931 (for those who don't remember, a sort of poor man's Marilyn Monroe – British film star and chat show circuit guest, who passed away in 1984). And Mark Lamarr. And every May the place is full of famous writers – at the well-respected Literary Festival.

Calne

A sweet spot now they've got rid of the massive Harris pig produce factory, which saw off 5,000 animals a week for sausages and pies. They have a lovely heritage centre in the old library, and lots of sculpture on the streets, including bronze pigs.

HOLIDAY INN EXPRESS

One of three Holiday Inns around here. The other two are in Swindon itself, one a proper Holiday Inn, the other an Express. We rang all three one Thursday evening in February to ask the cost of a single room the following night. The proper Inn price was £69, the downtown Express £79 and this one was just £44.95. Two celebs have stayed here: Pete Waterman and Charlotte Church. Yes, in different rooms on different nights.

CARDINAL HEALTH

UK HQ of a major manufacturer and distributor of medical products to hospitals. They've recently installed a machine that will turn out 75,000 pharmaceutical tablets an hour using photocopier technology, but their sales teams concentrate on single-use gowns, sterile procedure packs, genesis sterilisation containers, suction equipment, examination gloves, surgical clippers and impregnated scrub brushes.

MAN ERF

About one in twelve big lorries on the motorway are powered by a MAN ERF tractor unit. The UK logistics operation is based here. The units (that is the cabs and engines) are custom built in Munich and shipped here for pre-delivery inspections. Rudolf Diesel built his first engine for MAN in 1893, and ERF stands for Edward Richard Foden. The firm provide units to Sainsburys, TNT, Budweiser and Eddie Stobbart, and have become "preferred bidders" for the MoD.

BATLEYS

Lawrence Batley OBE was a cash and carry pioneer in Huddersfield in the 1960s. Originally called 'Come and Get It', the company now has 18 depots, mostly in the North of England, providing the trade with 25,000 lines. When we called they were doing twelve 550ml bottles of Newcastle Brown Ale for £10.39. Outside the manager's office is an ever-changing hand-written list of "Bad Suppliers". Reps wince to find their firm's name up there, and work hard to get it removed.

SWINDON'S OTHER RAILWAY

The Midland and South Western ran from Cirencester to Marlborough, and had its own Swindon station because they didn't get on with the GWR. The theory was it would provide a handy direct route from Manchester to Southampton, but it only really flourished during WW1 when used to ferry men and munitions from the north west to the south coast.

Track down Alan Jowett's colourful 'Railway Atlas' for a full "pre-grouping" picture.

HAY LANE SITE

There are 37 plots on what has been an English gypsy base for 30 years. The council supply a brick wash-shed, and occupiers place caravans or mobile chalets on the plot for which they pay a rent and council tax. Over 100 people live here operating a number of successful businesses, including flat roof repairs, landscaping, plastic and metal recycling and second-hand lorry exporting.

Despite the proximity of the motorway and railway, there's a long waiting list. Find out about contemporary Gypsy Travellers in 'Travellers Times' from the Rural Media Company (01432 344039).

DIDCOT-BATH/BRISTOL

Northward the track passes the old railway works before reaching Swindon station from where it goes towards Paddington.

Close to Swindon station is the GWR STEAM Museum. Next door are English Heritage's National Monuments Record office in an old GWR building, and new National Trust headquarters in new premises on the site of the boilermakers' workshops.

WHARF FARM

Originally a canal warehouse built around 1800. The current tenant farmer discovered three old shoes under the stairs: a man's, a woman's and a child's. Secreting a shoe from each family member in such a way was a custom by first occupants of houses at that time.

WROUGHTON AIRFIELD

On the plateau at the northern edge of the Marlborough Downs is a massive airfield which was a testing centre during WW2. 10,000 aircraft, including 500 helicopters, were initially flown from here. Now many of the hangars are full of wonderful inventions, because it's a storage facility for the Science Museum: 20,000 large devices that can't be kept in London, including some aircraft. Information and access is poor, though they did manage to be a venue for BBC Bristol's '20th Century Antiques', presented by top TV gardener Alan Titchmarsh.

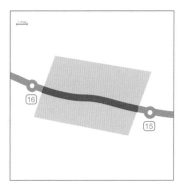

WAKEFIELD HOUSE (W.O.)

You've seldom seen swankier offices than these. And who would be able to occupy such grand premises? Only a company that knows its future is assured. And that would be a motor vehicle lubricant manufacturer.

On the strength of these facilities, it's clear that Castrol are invincible, luxuriating in the knowledge that every vehicle on this carriageway for evermore will need its share of their products and services.

NATIONWIDE

The world's largest building society has its Head Office tucked behind this tree-lined bank: 3,000 people in a white building powered by hydro-electricity. It's across the road from one of Swindon's well-run Park and Ride locations.

NIGHTINGALE FARM

Farmer Michael Hall has fond memories of the motorway construction crews who were "great guys". When the carriageways were first laid, Michael used them as a short cut, and when the M4 became operational, he continued doing so until he was stopped by the police and then fined for driving an unregistered tractor pulling an over-loaded trailer along the motorway.

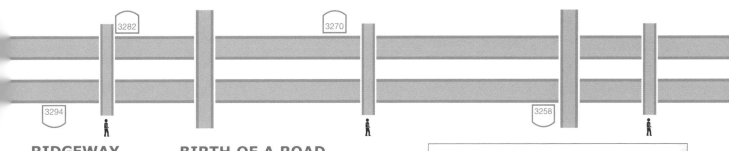

3294   3282   3270   3258

RIDGEWAY SCHOOL (E.O.)

This was Wiltshire's first purpose-built comprehensive school, opened in 1967. It's now a Foundation School with specialist status in science. To this end they are developing a 'Creative Planet Centre' with some help from the Wroughton Science Museum. "The School has high expectations of its pupils and they will be stretched." The 2004 pass rate at GCE A-level was 99%. ▼

BIRTH OF A ROAD

Wiltshire schools got a lot of mileage out of the arrival of the M4. Teachers made the appearance and impact of the motorway the subject of lots of projects, involving surveys, creative activities and reports, the major results of which were published by Hart-Davis Educational in 1973. This included a study of how farms might be affected by the carriageway, documented by Richard Mattick of Park School: "On the dull but not inclement Monday of half-term, we set out by car, bicycle and on foot to the farms we had each been allocated. We found that when approached in a polite and friendly way, the farmers were most helpful and soon gave us the facts we wanted to know." See, just like doing the M4 Sights Guide.

'SCOOTER' BRIDGE

This marks the eastern side of a circular 28 mile Millennium walking Trail through and south of Swindon, established by the Countryside Rangers. "Caring walkers take nothing but photos, leave nothing but footprints, kill nothing but time." We watched two kids ride their scooters down the northern double-loop side. It's perfect for such a purpose, and it must also look like the undercarriage of a scooter from above, so we've given it that name, which we hope will stick.

GREAT WESTERN HOSPITAL

A private finance initiative undertaking, this place opened in December 2002 and serves a population of around 300,000.

Last year the 3,300 Swindon and Marlborough NHS trust staff treated over 7,000 inpatients, 15,000 daycases and 20,000 emergency admissions.

They also saw 240,000 outpatients and helped 3,343 babies to be born.

There's a very good canteen, and if you can pass yourself off as a member of staff, you get served first and cheaper.

MOTORWAY COTTAGES

Planning Regulations were alerting locals to the proposed Swindon Gateway expansion "to include 1,430 residential units, a university campus, student accommodation, employment, shopping, and ancillary facilities.

LIDDINGTON CHURCH (W.O.)

The village's Post Office and General Stores closed in August 2004. But there's a village hall, opened in 1994 by the Duke of Marlborough, funded by Littlewoods, Vernons and Zetters. The hall, not the duke. In the 1830s the place was a hot bed of farm machine breaking, by poor workers demanding they be paid two shillings a day.

KING EDWARD'S PLACE

We can glimpse a gatehouse to an estate where it's believed King Edward VII (son of Victoria) used to rendezvous with Lillie Langtry for secret horse riding and other stuff.

Hence the place became informally known as King Edward's. Now it's known as Zurich's, because from within a collection of curious new buildings around the old we find the insurance firm's training centre.

ROMAN REMAINS

Mike Stone, Curator of Chippenham's Heritage Centre, kindly brought to our attention the frustrating undertakings by local archaeologists when the motorway construction contractors got stuck in to establishing Junction 15. A big group of Roman villas, bath houses and farm buildings was revealed, and the investigators struggled to gather detail of what lay down there as the earth-shifters thundered through. The endeavours are admirably documented in the Wiltshire Archaeological Magazine, that notes: "A complex series of rooms was rapidly destroyed," and "little datable material was obtained under the most distressing of archaeological circumstances."

BAD CHRISTMAS

A stocking filler for Scrooges — Mike Jackson

Britain's youngest drink-drinker took her uncle's car on to Swindon roads on Christmas Day "for a bit of a laugh". The 12 year old's breath test was nearly double the legal limit. Lots of seasonal laughs in our book of funny Christmas stories. Details on page 96.

SPIRIT OF SWINDON

Gillian Minter's winning local poem was blazoned across billboards in the town when we visited. She kindly agreed to us quoting a bit:
Before you spread your wings too far,
Before you travel on too fast,
Swindon, think of who you are:
Recollect your past.

Stone was quarried.
Merchants came.
Canals were built to carry coal.

But Swindon played a waiting game –
Kept its agricultural soul,
Till Daniel Gooch was sent to look,
And altered Swindon's history book.

Brunel built, the railway thrived,
The world of steam swamped old tradition.
Swindon township had survived
But changed beyond all recognition.

So as you tread your urban street,
Think what lies beneath your feet.

FOXHILLS MAST

This is next to the 136 km Ridgeway trail, running from Avebury to Tring.

"Persons fitted with heart pacemakers or similar devices are advised to avoid antenna installation areas."

HILLSIDE FARM

At a nearby outbuilding we learned we were being watched by Wiltshire Fire Brigade and that arson can carry a penalty of imprisonment. Down the road is the Shepherd's Rest where they do local venison.▼

RUSSLEY PARK
(E.O.)

These posh properties have replaced what was one of the country's finest horse stables with 45 superbly appointed separate units from where Sonny Hall trained dozens of winners, including 11 across a single weekend. The stables were built at the command of Lord Wavertree before WW1, apprentice builders walking from Swindon to work there.

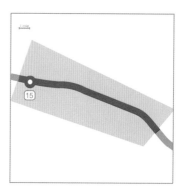

LODGE DOWN

You will not find a more pleasing place to spend a night along the M4 than this delightful country house on Ermin Street south of Lambourn. Lovely rooms, pleasant company and an excellent breakfast.

Phone Sally or John Cook on 01672 540304.

SETTING AN EXAMPLE

Harriet Harman, Solicitor General at the time, got stopped for doing 99 mph near here in January 2003. North Wiltshire magistrates gave her a £400 fine and banned her from driving for seven days. This year drivers mounted a go-slow protest at the number of speed cameras catching them from motorway bridges.

BIG FIELDS, BIG FARMS

The clumps of trees on the tops of the hills are growing in a clay cap on the otherwise chalky downs. Liddington Warren farm supplied rabbits to the table of Henry VIII.

Marlborough

I have fond memories of this delightful town as the halfway stop when taking or collecting my son Ben between home and college in Bournemouth. We'd have coffee in the Castle and Ball Hotel. I eventually got to stay there when making inserts for 'Flog It'. Paul Martin insisted we dined at Coles Restaurant opposite his flat. Fair dos. It was first class.

BAYDON WATER TOWER (W.O.)

This holds 570,000 litres, drawn from an underground aquifer and treated at Thames Water's Fognam Down plant at Lambourn. Amongst its beneficiaries is Baydon, the neighbouring highest village in Wiltshire. The well-supplied Stores (goose eggs £1) gains extra custom from through traffic when the motorway is closed between junctions 14 and 15, which happens about once a month. In the Red Lion we met Johnny Johnson, long time horse stables worker, who remembers the 30 feet high snow drifts of 1962/63, when rabbits would pop up and eat the

twigs off the top of the trees. Like his late brother, Johnny wants his ashes scattered on one of the horse gallops, many of which these days have been ploughed up into commercial farm land.

MEMBURY MAST

This was built in 1965 to transmit 405-line black and white TV pictures. Now it's NTL's very useful structure for positioning microwave dishes and mobile phone antennas.

To the west is an intensive pig unit next to Membury Pallets, who collect the one-journey pallets that carry food to Iceland and M&S depots, and sell on 2,000 of them a week to other users.

MEMBURY EAST

"Coach Drivers when calling in a professional capacity are invited to eat in any of our food outlets for the nominal charge of 1p. Excludes McDonalds."

Wantage

For Festival of Britain celebrations, in 1951 Collins produced a series of 13 guide books About Britain. No. 5 is the least convincing entity: Chilterns to Black Country, W.G. Hoskins struggling to find a commonality from such diverse parts. At the back are illustrated country motoring tours. "Wantage: The birth-place of Alfred the Great and now a sleepy and unpretentious market town of some charm."

ARENA

It's all about bums on seats. The racking store rows of plastic seating that are ferried out to public and private events around the country. If you've been to Robot Wars or Formula One, chances are you sat on one.

DIXON'S FARM LORRY COMPOUND

At the other end of the lane is the swanky Hare restaurant. Starters were 8 – 10 (they don't bother with shillings, or pound signs), The charming manager recommended the terrine of foie gras, chicken liver mousse, raisin puree and brioche. We said we didn't eat meat, so the award-winning chef knocked us up a tasty dollop of mushroom risotto with a poached egg in batter plonked on top. That was just 15, whereas their other main courses came in at 19+, and that was without vegetables, salad or potatoes (all at 3). We didn't examine the dessert menu but nipped up to Lambourn Co-op where we got 6 Cherry Bakewells for 89p.

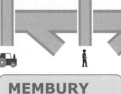

MEMBURY WEST

We're in the middle of what was a WW2 airfield from where 90 aircraft took off on 5th June 1944 to drop parachutists over Cherbourg. To the south, there's still a strip where Angus Fleming test flies his own designs of light aircraft. We met him working on the Magnum that, once certificated, will do 160 knots from 100 horsepower. To the east is an old hanger full of "a selective broad spectrum bactericidal agent and acidifier for pig feeds".

RUTPEN (E.O.)

These are chemicals processing and refining plants. Most successful product? Detergent. We were shown the thick file of solicitors' letters that documented the change of use of the land from farming to airfield to motorway route and factory units. Complicated. The lawyers must have loved it.

INDUSTRIAL ACCIDENTS

We tend to think of injuries at work as likely in factories or down mines. In these parts, where horse training is big business, The Racing Welfare News headlined the case of a trainer's travelling head girl who had suffered a bad fall that had left her paralysed from the armpits downward.

Hungerford

"Crowded with vehicles and foot passengers" on the Great Western road, there was frequent whipping of vagrants or vagabonds "by stripping them naked from the middle upwards, and causing them to be lashed until their bodies be bloody, in the presence of the minister of the parish." In 1692 the Town Sergeant was given five shillings "for his extraordinary paines this year and whipping of severall persons."

These days you can take a trip along the Kennet and Avon aboard the Rose of Hungerford.

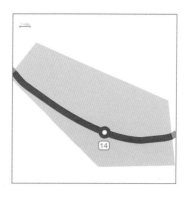

WOODLAND ST MARY

We roar past glimpses of this village on Ermin Street, which, under the Countryside Stewardship Scheme, has set up some permissive paths for walkers, and has enhanced the hedgerows and grass margins of cultivated fields to provide over-wintering habitats for birds and insects. Across the motorway, literally, by bridge, is the sniffy Inholmes estate, once occupied by the Gilbey Gin family and now home to Frank Williams of Formula One motor racing fame.

MINI VMS

Aren't these Variable Message Signs nice and neat? And they can do colour pictograms. We wrote to Alastair Darling last year about the big, ugly, previous generation signs that look like something off the decks of aircraft carriers. Robert Ridgeway, SSR SID SSMG TST, of the Highways Agency, replied to say he would provide a comprehensive response shortly. He didn't. We rang up the Helpline. They'd never heard of him and didn't know what the letters after his name stood for.

NO JUSTICE

Pity the poor Puxleys. They've had it tough. Irish Republicans burnt down their castle in Cork, so they had to squeeze on to the 5,000 acre Welford Park estate, (picked up through a series of judicious marriages and handy inheritances). Blow me, if the Ministry of Defence didn't demand a chunk of it, after which the Department of Transport took away a bit more. And so now they suffer the relentless growl of the motorway to their south.

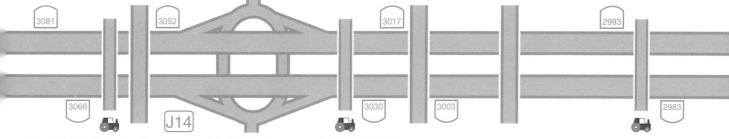

FAKE FARMERS

A big farm at Lower Poughley is being turned into lots of listed barn conversions. Day-glo notices proclaimed that "no further publicity will normally be given to any modifications unless a further application is needed." The prospect was not seen as good news by some neighbours.

They feared the influx of townies in 4x4s. 60,000 such 2+ tonne, 22-gallon vehicles were sold back in 1993. By last year, the figure had jumped to 175,000, accounting for nearly 6% of new vehicles purchased. 'What Car' magazine made the "family-friendly" £33,000 Land Rover Discovery it's Car of the Year. The Alliance against Urban 4x4s regularly protests outside dealerships with the slogan "Not safe, not clean, not cool."

ORANGE BOXES

Ian Beck of Highways Agency Traffic Technology went to great lengths to explain to us the numbering system for the M4: A figure of 2000 is the base point somewhere near the centre of London. The middle two digits represent distance in kilometres from that point, the fourth digit being tenths of a kilometre; and he faxed us Volume 9 Section 5 Part 1 Annex A of the Design Manual for Roads and Bridges to prove it.

WICKHAM

Council houses thru the trees indicate this village where, in April 2005, Lib Dem posters were out in force to offset the Tory banners of Welford to the north.

A.W. Garvey, a previous clerk of Welford Parish, that embraces Wickham, did a great History and a well-illustrated map of the area a few years ago.

PORK SCRATCHINGS

Above the hamlet of Easton (where Sovereign are re-building houses, and the agricultural machinery depot does a roaring trade) are hundreds of free range pigs.

Nearby we discovered an empty bag of Bartholomew's Gamecock Feed: "an economical, attractive and palatable feed enticing birds into areas where wheat alone may fail. Small seeds, maize and pellets, the mixture is an irresistible attraction to pheasants."

Didcot Railway Centre

Our accountant Chris Burnley (who has generously advised us on railway matters) was insistent we make it clear that here you can see a replication of a length of Brunel's original seven feet wide gauge line, complete with a working locomotive modelled on a GWR original.

WORKS UNIT ONLY

If you come off the carriageway here you soon reach a padlocked gate before the line of telegraph poles. Nearby we came across a pub promoting bottles of Veuve Cliquot as 'exceptional value at £34.95." Really? And further east we found this sweet old barn in a sea of oil seed rape - evidence of the Puxleys farming on a jumbo scale.

NATIONAL EXPRESS

You won't go far along the M4 without passing a National Express coach.

Across the country there are 540 of them operating between 1,000 destinations and carrying 16 million customers a year. We paid £14 for a round trip from Swindon to London's Victoria coach station via Heathrow.

Excellent value and a clean, comfortable vehicle. "A proud heritage of public transport that goes back well over 100 years". We commend them to you.

CRABS

Fish restaurant with loads of old lobster pots and new BMWs, Mercs and Jags outside. We were very impressed with a topiary horse with a huge erection, balancing itself on the end of its willy stuck in the ground. But this was a misunderstanding. The animal wasn't taking its whole weight on its penis. A passer-by explained that the trunk of the tree was not part of the foliage sculpture.

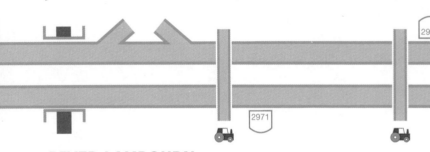

RIVER LAMBOURN

This comes down the 'Valley of the Racehorse' and passes through Welford Park before reaching here and then the Kennet at Newbury. At Welford In Victorian times they diverted the water into a turbine in the Laundry to generate electricity.

WINTERBOURNE

Remember the Avengers? Patrick McNee as Steed, and various glamorous actresses in Rolls Royces. We were reminded of that world when we came here. People were secretive. Reluctant to admit to what they knew. Lots of fancy old houses, some with CCTV or guard dogs, others displaying St George flags or croquet sets. Some farm buildings in decay, other hi-tech. New gravestones for members of the big landowning dynasties. The pub landlord in a black shirt saying he was new to the area.

IBS JOINERY (E.O.)

In Wyfield Manor's old tractor shed a couple of guys do customised door and window frames for a firm in Reading.

The local garden show was inviting entries for tallest sunflower, biggest onion, heaviest marrow and fattest leek. "Start growing now."

WESTBROOK (W.O.)

This hamlet is another place where the farming's gone industrial, leaving buildings for private use or business. Here we found upholstery and security firms. Ditchfield's 1893 Tourist Guide to Berkshire records that a man stole a sheep near here and tied it round his neck by its legs. It struggled and pulled him to the ground, strangling him to death.

We like to solve mysteries, but we thought we'd leave this one for you.

Oxford

If you want to be Prime Minister, you've got to study in these parts, statistically-speaking. Most No 10 occupants did time in the town. We were partially educated here. We once had a golf lesson at the Oxfordshire, whilst making 'Tim Brooke-Taylor's Golf Clubs' for Discovery. We witnessed the old Goodie's game improve at each course, and eventually gave him a camera to film us applying what we'd picked up watching some of the country's best pros on their home patches.

BRIDLEWAY BRIDGE

A sop to the locals whilst remodelling Junction 13. Costains closed the motorway overnight in March 2004 to take the old bridge away, then closed it again one July night to put this one in place. The 40 mile speed limit during the construction period resulted in the prosecution of 1,000 vehicles in May 2004.

A34

After seeing off all those horrible hippy types who'd made their life a misery over the Newbury bypass, continuing the chalk cutting northward beyond the M4 was a piece of cake. All they had to do was dig underneath the motorway, moving 900,000 cubic metres of material, and deploying 13,000 cubic metres of concrete and 1,300 tonnes of steel.

Newbury Showground

The Agricultural Society run competitions that includes the Thames and Kennett Machinery Ring Trophy for Best Winter Oil Seed Rape. It costs £5.88 to enter, which guarantees an invite to a farm walk and bar-b-que at last year's Best Farmed Farm Champion Farm – Welford, by kind permission of James Puxley.

J13

BUSSOCK WOOD

We attended the annual May Bank Holiday garden party (supporting local charities) and met William Palmer, once technical director at Reading's famous biscuit factory. He bought the 100 acres, with a big 1907 house in the middle, in the 1960s, not long before it was decided to lay the M4 along here, which was "a blow".

CHIEVELEY SERVICES

Chieveley the place is at the opposite corner of Junction 13. In AD951, King Edred gave Chieveley to his servant Wulfric, then took it back again. The Parish Evaluation questionnaire asks: "Do you help with activities locally (e.g. Fete, Flower Festival, Plant & Produce Sale, Magazine Distribution, Collecting for Charity, Carols for Everyone, Church Music, Churchyard Maintenance, Church Services & Events. Yes or No?."

SCHOOL OF MILITARY SURVEY (E.O.)

This is where Royal Engineer Officers undertake their Master of Science degrees in Defence Geographic Information. It's part of the Army Survey Course which also turns out Geographic Military Engineer Data and Terrain Analyst Technicians.

They announced an open day, and we turned up to discover bouncy castles, tombolas and home made jam. Em, it was just a sort of play day for local community organisations. And we'd been looking forward to exchanging military secrets about map design. Don't suppose a motorway sights guide would be much use in Kosovo or Bosnia which is where the 42 Engineer Regiment have been operating recently.

Newbury

Let's face it, the most famous thing about this place is its bypass. Formidable efforts were made by thousands who disliked the chosen route or opposed the very notion of a huge scar through the countryside to relieve the town from traffic.

Friends of the Earth co-ordinated protesters, many of whom camped out along the route of the proposed road, and were condemned as "rent-a-mob hippy eco-warriors." In February 1996 the offices of Tarmac were wrecked by 60 demonstrators. It was believed some were on the dole and others were being secretly supported by wealthy locals with an interest in inhibiting the route.

Now Newbury has a vision for its town centre – to be completed by 2025.

THE BOYS DONE GOOD

Back in the 1880s, little Eddie Iliffe produced a popular magazine called Bicycle News. In 1891 Willy Iliffe launched the Midland Evening Telegraph, and a few years later followed that up with Autocar, based in Coventry.

In 1924 Iliffe and Sons bought Wireless World, reckoning it might be a goer.

In 1933, Eddie was made a member of the House of Lords. In 1944 the Iliffes bought up a bunch of Midlands newspaper including the Birmingham Post. In 1987, Lord Iliffe sold the Birmingham Post and Mail for £60m. The current Lord Iliffe inherited the title from his uncle in 1996 and is ranked 247 in the Sunday Times Rich List with £170m under his belt, and now he lives just along the road.

WHERE'S THE MONEY COME FROM?

A Dreweatt Neate agent explained to us that 20 years ago 80% of income from the land in these parts came from producing food. Now that proportion is just 20%, the balance deriving from "other activities".

GUIDE TO SAFER MOTORWAY DRIVING

The Department of Transport ask us to use the 2 second rule. It should take at least 2 seconds for you to reach the point where the vehicle in front of you is now. Driving when you are tired greatly increases your accident risk. If you break down, pull in as far to the left of the hard shoulder as possible with your wheels turned to the left.

Don't use your mobile to call for assistance. It's hard for you and the person at the other end to work out exactly where you are, whereas the orange emergency phone (at one mile intervals) will identify your precise location.

COMMON BARN COTTAGES

"We do not buy or sell at this door. And require no free advice, thank you. Identification is required from unknown callers." A selection of old Austin cars on the front lawn plus a Harmony caravan.

YOU THINK IT'S BAD HERE?

Last year 4 million cars were bought by people in China. That annual figure is projected to rise to 7 million by 2010. And whereas 3,000 people die in motor accidents in the UK each year, in China the World Health Organisation estimates the fatalities from road accidents to be in excess of 500 per day.

GO COLD

Near here a lady gave us an environmental tip: In hotels and restaurants, don't reach for the hot tap. Save energy by going for cold.

PRIORS COURT COTTAGES

There are cottages along the lane both sides of the motorway, some blighted by proximity to the now-closed Hermitage landfill site (behind the pile of earth to the north that will be used for landscaping). Nearby we met ex-cruise ship photographer Tim Wild cleaning out his stretch limo converted to LPG for economy. Good Coffee House at the Hillier Garden Centre.

STOP LINE

There are dozens of pill boxes round here, built in 1940 when Churchill reckoned England might be invaded by the Germans. It was believed the Kennet and Avon Canal could work as an anti-tank ditch.

HERMITAGE FARM, OARE

They keep cereals and chemicals here, plus sophisticated kit for testing soil to create an electronic grid record of the characteristics of each field, and what additives should be applied to any specific patch season by season to maximise growing capabilities.

IS THAT A MAST?

Clever old Vodaphone, eh! Sick of lattice structures spoiling the landscape? Now you can have your very own comms mast cleverly disguised as a run-of-the-mill conifer.

NO BOOK?

When we first surveyed the M4 we were worried there wasn't enough round here to make it viable. You see it's all a matter of getting off the beaten track and politely making enquiries.

BUGGER OFF

We asked two ladies in Frilsham what was the most interesting thing about the village. They said the Well, and directed us to it in the woods, but we got lost and so asked a couple gardening for further directions. They told us to "bugger off", but their neighbours were most helpful. Unimpressed by the brick box with water in the bottom, we then found for ourselves the Pot Kiln pub and the excellent, award-winning products of its West Berkshire micro-brewery.

NO CHANGE THERE THEN

Lots of trees mean lots of clay, and so the only cash crop is Christmas trees, of which the enormous Yattendon estate, owned by Lord Iliffe, churns out 150,000 a year. He owns most of the village too, including the Royal Oak where we had a "special" Sunday afternoon cream tea (current bun with jam, marmalade and cream, supplied with quality cutlery) for £7.50. Yep, £7.50. And the good Lord has been getting £300,000 from the government in farming subsidies each year. But we got a smashing piece of cheddar in the shop for just £2.55.

There are nearly 9,000 acres altogether, of which 2,000 is woodland. They're got 20 staff on the estate, and 12 on the farms, and they "look after" 27 pensioners.

THAT'S A TREE?

Go on, admit it. You've passed this spot hundreds of times and not realised that was a plastic sheath over a metal structure.

Beale Park

Halfway between Reading and Goring, this home to lots of exotic birds and animals was hosting the Thames Boat Show for the third time in June 2005. You could get there by taking a train to Pangbourne, then a ferry from the Swan pub.

2860 2831 2809

2844 2819 2799

RIVER PANG

It rises at East Isley (north of the Newbury showground) and swings south, then north again to reach the Thames at Pangbourne. More than 20 types of wild flowers can be found along the valley, if you know what to look for.

BIRCH COTTAGE

This sits on the Eling estate that was owned by a Huntley Palmer: Gerald, who had no offspring and so set up a trust of which one of the greatest beneficiaries is the Greek Orthodox Church.

COXLANDS
(W.O.)

This was a Yattendon property which they sold on to Trinity College, Cambridge, which then passed it on elsewhere. Great view of some Christmas tree plantations.

DEER LOOSE

Hundreds of deer die from road accidents in the UK each year, and those same accidents kill 10 motorists and injure 300. One little deer became trapped in a car's front bumper and was carried 20 miles before the driver realised. She was extracted in one piece and returned to the woods. We took a wander through some woods near here and encountered a delightful roe deer that moved with extraordinary speed when it detected us. Beyond our comprehension how people can shoot them.

BARN ELM DIRT TRACK

This no-longer-used facility was a motorway construction site, where workers were always on the lookout for Roman remains. One morning a digger driver discovered some curious coins. They were taken to Reading University archaeology department and identified as 1966 World Cup souvenir gilt medallions.

TIDMARSH MANOR

Once home of the Leynhams who, in 1544, coughed up for a fancy Bible for the church. This "made its way" in 1935 to a London dealer, who persuaded the locals to raise £128 for its return.

RIVER PANG

Further downstream is well-heeled Pangbourne, with a huge Bentley dealership, and Parish Council assets of half a million. We had an excellent value spaghetti lunch at the Mia Beni restaurant in the George Hotel.

PARK LANE TOWER

Constructed by Reading Corporation to hold 200,000 gallons for the people of Tilehurst. Inaugurated by Alderman Felix Parfitt J.P., Chairman of the Waterworks Committee in October 1932.

PIGEON TOWER

In the 1780s, the Lord of the Manor of Sulham fancied an up-market bird from Sulhamstead a few miles away, and so he built this on his hill so she could see it from her bedroom window and thus be impressed by his manliness. We don't know if it worked.

WATER EXTRACTION WORKS (W.O.)

A bore hole here provided Reading with its water until more elaborate systems were set up over in Pangbourne to the north west.

Down the road is a Homebase, with an even bigger silver shed round the corner housing the Reading Porsche dealership.

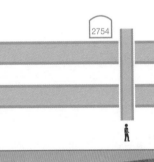

MALPAS BARNS

The sheds by the scooter footbridge are part of the Copas empire. This enterprising family, based in Cookham, bought a lump of land at Henley which gave them unrivalled facilities for entertaining Royal Regatta visitors. Rest of the year they do turkeys.

CAN WE COUNT ON YOUR SUPPORT?

Conservative candidate for Newbury Richard Benyon had hundreds of posters peppering the county at the start of May 2005. Of course, when your family owns lots of the land, you have more places to put those banners. And you can rely on your tenants to display a flyer in their front window, though that doesn't mean they're going to vote for you. Richard's the latest in a long line of Benyons to inherit the extensive and elaborate Englefield estate and an appetite for politics. And those banners worked.

ARLINGTON BUSINESS PARK

Royal Bank of Scotland have an outpost here opposite Vodaphone's network planning engineers.

MOST HOLY TRINITY, THEALE (W.O.)

Local architect Edward Garbett designed this in 1820 but died before it was finished. It's considered by Mark Chatfield to be one of the most important early 19th century Gothic Revival churches in England. Constable painted it and Brunel prayed in it.

BURGHFIELD MILL

You can get an apartment here (starting at £250,000) by calling Mann the estate agents, or you can get a drink up the road at the Cunning Man, on the east bank of the canal.

TOPMIX

Gravel extraction continues from these Berry's Lane pits. Down the road another hole is being filled in with crush concrete and other building site rubbish by J. Mould and co. Lots of the old gravel lakes are used for fishing; one boasts a fly fishing store and casting school: 2 sessions on spey casting for £140.

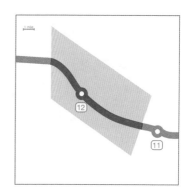

KIRTON FARM HOTEL

Once you've found it, you'll love the massive koi carp in the ornamental pond, and look out for Human Table Football in a sort of bouncy castle outside the Club.

READING-NEWBURY

A few miles south west is where, in November 2004, depressed chef Brian Drysdale parked his Mazda on a level crossing, derailing a Plymouth express and killing six passengers.

READING EAST

"Please remember to pay for your fuel." Images are being recorded for the purpose of crime prevention and public safety, with number plate recognition cameras.

KENNET AND AVON CANAL

This opened in 1810, linking Reading to Bristol. It's 87 miles long with 104 locks, and it flourished until GWR came along in 1841. The Kennet River makes up part of the waterway.

READING WEST

You know those Admedia panels in the toilets. To occupy one space costs £90 per panel for 4 weeks, and nationally that would expose you to 27.6 million men.

READING-BASINGSTOKE

Track down the publications of Two Rivers Press, based in Reading, for some delightful insights into the town and its history. They do an Ancient Boundary Map, and an anthology of local and visitor opinions since 1686, entitled 'A Much-maligned Town'.

BURGHFIELD SAILING CLUB

Around 400 dinghies live here, making it one of the largest inland clubs, but they have got 200 acres of water on which to manoeuvre; and a couple of sailors are especially good at that because on weekdays they assemble components for submarines.

Theale

Goaman and Every's social survey of 1894 to 1965 recorded that the first commercial motor vehicle in Theale was Carter's adapted Model T Ford that could only climb steep hills in reverse. It's now got a smart-looking main street with plenty of pubs and a friendly Co-op. Lots of pleasant frontages are featured in their Millennium Community Quilt, that's captured in a cute pocket book.

300 LONGWATER AVENUE, GREEN PARK

Heading east, this is the first empty office building visible on an estate created by the Prudential to accommodate Cisco Systems shortly prior to the dotcom collapse. Cisco are elsewhere on the complex, and paying all their bills. They just don't need as many offices as they thought they would.

400/450 SOUTH OAK WAY

The place is peppered with security staff, even though there's nothing to nick. But you don't want kids breaking the glass, do you.

MADEJSKI STADIUM

Alan Sedunary's 'A to Z of Reading Football Club' contains more than one Death. First Steve, their 1970s goalkeeper; then the demise of a number of players and fans at various incidents on and off the pitch. Chairman John Madejski made his money from creating Auto Trader, and now generously supports local institutions. Who said they thought it was an East European personal watercraft?

300 SOUTH OAK WAY

"The most successful companies are coming to recognise that, as a source of inspiration, few things are more important than the quality of their working environment."

BIT OF A BLOW

A 120 metre high wind turbine is soon to be erected here. Some environmentalists estimate it would do the planet more good to cancel one daily passenger service between Heathrow and Florida for a year.

2668

ROADSIDE REMEMBRANCE

Near here we encountered a lady looking for the memorial garden she'd established in a hedgerow. It commemorated a police officer killed in an accident whilst guarding a missile convoy en route for Coulport in Scotland.

LAGOONA PARK

This is where some of Reading's new rich come to play with their personal jet ski toys. Not a place where environmental good practice is high on the agenda. But we've roared big engines across water, so we know it's great fun.

They're open 7 days a week from 10.30 am until dusk.

You get the feeling that the Green Party is unlikely to ever get much traction in these parts.

Reading

Best approach to the centre is on foot from Prospect Park, so you can walk down the Bath Road and appreciate its fine buildings. You eventually reach the checkerboard tower of St. Mary's, where you can turn left (north) and head for the delights of the main shopping streets. For lunchtime eating you will not do better than the John Lewis department store food court. Soup, coffee and a fruits of the forest pancake with ice cream for under a tenner.

Predictably, for the Antiques Roadshow, we were including a sequence about Oscar Wilde in Reading gaol, which gave me and cameraman John Hunter the chance of a guided tour. This was our first time in prison. As the Governor enthused about the external brickwork, John and I were transfixed by a small paper cone being lowered from an open top floor window down to the first floor on the end of a piece of string. A hand emerged from the first floor window and popped a cigarette into the paper cone, which was then hauled up again.

Huntley and Palmer workers used to view executions from the roof of their factory, we were told by someone who knows.

Reading University is a centre of excellence for all things agricultural from land use to food technology, and its museum has a great range of farming artefacts.

ORACLE

A "medium or agency of divine revelation; a person with the repute or air of infallibility or great wisdom." Chambers Twentieth Century Dictionary. Alas, this one's nowt but a shopping arcade. And regards infallibility, beware their maps in Reading town centre, positioning the Tourist Information Office at the Town Hall, where it hasn't been for five years since it moved behind St. Mary's.

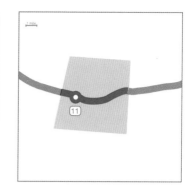

SCOTTISH COURAGE BREWERY

Fosters, Kronenbourg 1664 and Miller beer comes out of here – 25 million pints in a week, providing jobs for 450, and £10 million a month in excise duty.

The process begins with the extraction of 100 litres of water a second from 200 metre deep boreholes below the 55 acre site.

MCI

You're looking at the remains of the world. That is, Worldcom, the outrageous American internet/communications outfit that fiddled its books and eventually got found out. MCI has millions of phone user customers, mostly in the States, which is why it's recently been bought by Colorado's Verizon for £4 billion.

FOSTER WHEELER

They do design, engineering, construction and project management for the refining, chemical, pharmaceutical and power industries.

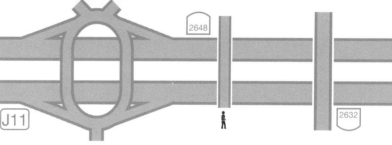

GOING NOWHERE?

To get our snap of MCI we took the unfriendly footpath down the side of the motorway, where we met a teenager who told us he'd walked from Basingstoke, but couldn't find his way back. We pointed out the A33 and gave him £4 for a bus fare. An hour later we spotted him here near Hartley's Court (of which we can see the top half) being given yet more directions. We resisted the temptation to ask him for our money back.

IN A HURRY

Lots of hyped up motorists in these parts. We witnessed a prang at Junction 11: young man in an open-top Super-Mini (Maxim nudes on his passenger seat) clipped by a Peugeot screeching round a corner.

Next day we tentatively crossed Junction 12 at 8.30 in the morning and were blared at by an MG for not going flat out (Yes, you, you prat!). Many are unaccommodating, unforgiving, seeking every advantage. What's the hurry? Anxieties about not getting rich enough quick enough? Or urgent messages in their ear-piece phones? Even the learner drivers are pushy. Can't be healthy.

Basingstoke

We only knew one thing about this place – that it was where Saddam Hussein got his giant ornamental sword archway from. Then something else cropped up to enrich our knowledge - a couple of drunks crashed their BMW into a bedroom – they were going so fast the car took off and made a big hole in the side of a house at first floor level. The Tourist Office couldn't tell us where the giant Iraqi swords were made, or where the house with a hole in it was located, but they did say we should include the Milestones Transport Museum in our book. It's got an excellent collection of Thornycroft agricultural and commercial vehicles built in the town in the 1930s.

Bracknell

"A small thoroughfare hamlet, adorned with many genteel residences and delightful villas," explained Pigot's Commercial Directory of 1830. "Letters for London and the Staines cross-post are dispatched at half-past six o'clock in the evening."

It became one of Britain's new towns in the 1950s, but the magic's worn off and now it's about to be re-built again, in a fashion that the designers hope will meet with approval from Prince Charles, who apparently doesn't care for the current version. Not that he's planning to move here, as far as we know.

WHAT TO SAY, WHAT TO SHOW?

We did an Antiques Roadshow at the Loddon Valley Leisure Centre here in Lower Earley. Strictly it's in Wokingham, but we reckoned the audience would expect to see images of Reading, which is mostly what they got. How do you decide what to say and shoot about somewhere that will be seen by 10 million, but not irritate the locals? Good training for these Guides, though, as you've noticed, we don't always apply it.

ABLE

If you've got some manufacturing process that needs sophisticated mechanical monitoring, then chances are these people have the solution. They can do instruments to measure level, flow, pressure, temperature, moisture, gas analysis, liquid analysis, density and light.

RIVER LODDON

This rises near Basingstoke and makes its way northward through Dinton Pastures Park (with excellent Countryside Services) to enter the Thames at Wargrave south of Henley. Kids occasionally swim in here, but they are exceptional. As the Royal Berkshire Life magazine points out: "The ownership of a swimming pool is within the reach of the majority."

WINNERSH TRIANGLE

This industrial estate sits at the end of the northern arm of the A329(M) running between Reading and Bracknell. In the triangle we find a huge regional depot for Royal Mail's Parcel Force, and a contact centre for our friends NTL, who employ 300 people here.

READING-WOKINGHAM

The line to the north once linked to a complex network of sidings within the 24 acre Huntley and Palmer biscuit factory. Joseph Huntley had been making cakes in Reading since 1822 and found plenty of custom from passengers on the London-Bath stage coaches. George Palmer joined him and encouraged a move towards mechanisation and longlife products, hence the biscuits. 500 people were working in the biscuit factory in 1860, turning out 3,000 tons a year in 100 different shapes. By the end of the century they had their own fleet of railway locomotives.

Wokingham

W. J. Gotelee was a Printer, Bookseller and Stationer in the Market Place, who each year produced a Compendium of the District "presented gratis to Customers." In 1912, this included the objectives of the Agricultural Association: "to encourage sober, honest and industrious farm servants and labourers in husbandry, which excites a spirit of industry among the labouring classes."

UPPERWOOD FARM

Not so much a farm as what's left of one. At the gate, on a sign surrounded by piles of rubbish, Wokingham District Council point out "Illegal fly tipping costs. See it, report it." The Wokingham Residents Environmental Guide is half advertising (Do your dentures make you look older?) and half free tips: "Don't leave fridge doors open". "Remember to put a plug in a basin".

HATCH FARM STABLES (E.O.)

This old cow shed is now an indoor training ring for the people who keep their horses in the livery. They were soon to have a visit from Joy West, List 3 British Dressage judge. She was going to spend the day offering tips for test riding. £20 to take part. There are 600,000 registered horses in the UK. Here's a question for you: what happens to horses when they die?

MITSUBISHI (W.O.)

The rust-coloured shed is where Reading's Mitsubishis are serviced. Shoguns are big on carbon dioxide emissions, fuel consumption, insurance premiums and servicing costs, according to What Car? If ever a ceiling should be placed on disposable income, it's surely when machines like these have become common currency.

MONKEY MATES

It's a kids' activity centre with well defined rules: "The party entitles you to 45 minutes in our Themed Party Room with unlimited squash. Parents are expected to bring their own Birthday Cake and Candles. We can supply filled party bags of sweets/ toys etc. Monkey Mates is not a Childcare Facility." Parents have to sign a personal responsibility form if their kids can't manage without wearing their spectacles. ▼

ALL WEATHER GALLOP

Bill Hill Park was cut in half by the motorway. The occupants breed race horses and established this dedicated track for training, but it's on clay so it doesn't work properly when it's been very dry or very wet.

We're getting close to polo land, where expensive horses are kept in expensive stables to ride in a few matches in the brief expensive season.

Maidenhead

"The loud handbag and daring leopard skin shoes said it all – she was on her way to a convincing victory. Theresa May certainly knows how to pick an outfit to match the event," reported the Slough Observer on 6th May 2005.

Symantec, the anti-virus wonks, sponsor a roundabout in town, so while you're waiting for their software to filter an e-mail, think of the pleasure you're giving Maidenhead's motorists. Question: why can't the filtering be done centrally, instead of on everyone's machine for £40 a year? Maidenhead will be the western end of the new Crossrail service from Essex, though many of the locals don't like the look of it. That doesn't include our compliance lawyer, Jonathan Holder.

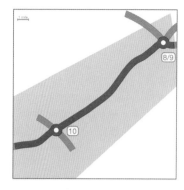

Henley

It's got a museum dedicated to the river and rowing, on the Thames 180 mile Path.

BEENHAM HEATH WATER TREATMENT WORKS

Through the trees we can briefly glimpse this plant that was established in the 1920s to provide drinking water to the people of Bracknell and Wokingham.

It recently had a £1 million micro-filtration unit fitted and currently pours out 32 million litres of water each day.

4 MILES

2506　2476　J9　J8

2559　2491　2462

KEEP OUT

We encountered secrecy and misinformation round here. Electronic gates and unanswered squawk boxes keep strangers at bay, and farm managers misled us about the heritage of their land. There's a gap in our layout along the four mile stretch east of here, which allows us to contemplate for a few minutes about what it is they're trying to hide.

THAMES TURF

These people struggled to suppress their sarcasm at how "fascinating" a book about the M4 might be. Let's face it, if you grow grass for a living, you know all about fascinating.

IN THE MONEY

The long corridor of trees is a tiny part of a huge estate owned by the Smiths of Shottesbrooke, a family whose wealth management goes back to the Exchequer of Henry VIII. Ex-Conservative MP, director of Coutts Bank and High Sheriff of Maidenhead, John Smith set up the Landmark Trust in the 1960s so the less privileged can pay to spend the odd night in a swanky house.

WANT A WEE?

The Highways Agency have been trying to negotiate the establishment of a new motorway service area in these parts, for which we were told the compensation could be in the region of £2 million, but that's cut no ice with the locals, one of whom is Michael Parkinson.

LORD SNOOTY & HIS PALS

The Royal Oak at Paley Street is very proud to have been the plotting platform for the Hooray Henry hunt fanatics who burst on to the floor of the House of Commons in September 2004, demonstrating their contempt for the meritocracy of Parliament.

MOOR FARM

We can just see the outbuildings behind an Elizabethan house that has been owned by a string of distinguished families to this day. In the early 18th century it was occupied by George Proctor, Keeper of the Seals and Courts of Record for Windsor Castle. Moor Farm does very good B&B and has cottages to let. It's in Holyport, that had a pub once called The Eagle, but renamed The Belgian after WW1 prisoners started saluting the sign outside.

PRINT DIRECT

Many of the glossy leaflets that get shoved through Maidenhead letterboxes are produced here.

DUCK OUT

You're passing over Bray, where we were once taken to lunch by Gerry 'Thunderbirds' Anderson in his Rolls Royce, before seeing rows of disposable razors being stuck on model rockets at Bray Studios for 'Space 1999'. The Jesus Hospital was founded in 1627 "to provide for the poore people for ever" and now has a sign outside saying: 'Vagrants, Hawkers and Dogs are not admitted'. Why did Heston Blumenthal stick his Fat Duck here ("the world's best restaurant") when there's a serious shortage of parking at the best of times? The cheap evening meal is just £65. A Windsor Castle warden told us that the service is superb. Would hope so.

High Wycombe

The footballers' wives here are drop dead gorgeous. This was where we made the first of many short sports films for Pebble Mill's 'Really Useful Show' with Adrian Goldberg. This one was about soccer match day crèches, and we struggled to concentrate whilst surrounded by the young Mums married to the players.

PRICE GLASS

They've been providing Maidenhead and Slough with glaziers and glass for 30 years.

TECHNICAL MOULDINGS

They make plastic injection components for cars and power tools, not least door handles and hammer drill casings.

RIVER THAMES

Mr and Mrs S.C. Hall produced an illustrated 'Book of the Thames' in 1859. Of this bit they said: "The land is fertile in themes, and the water is hardly less so; the barges, the punts, the gay wherries, the racing-boats are everywhere; and perhaps in no part of the world are there to be obtained enjoyments so many or so full."

JUBILEE RIVER

The Environment Agency have created this 11 kilometre, £50 million artificial river parallel to the Thames flowing from Maidenhead to Datchet to draw off a proportion of the waters of the real river as a means of lessening flood risks. The M4 was diverted for months on end to allow them to cut the channel. They've even put in little islands for nesting terns and little ringed plovers.

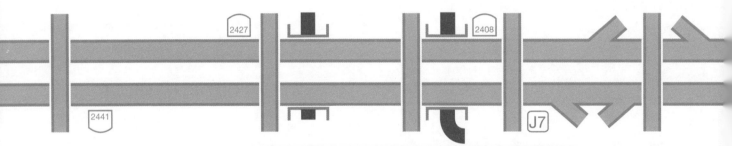

DISFIGUREMENTS

In 1929 the Earl of Mayo saw fit to commission a survey of the state of the Thames Valley. Regards these parts he warned "the river front should be watched carefully to guard against its exploitation for shacks and similar disfigurements." Immediately downstream are the Monkey Island hotel, Bray Marina and Bray Lake Watersports, all very pleasing.

SPLASH OUT

You want a tiptop rowing team but the Thames is increasingly full of motor boats, fishing lines and sewage, so what do you do? Dig out a rectangular hole 2,000 metres long and 8 lanes wide and call it Dorney Lake. That's what Eton College have done, and you can be sure more Olympic gold medals will be heading this way due to their audacious and spectacular investment.

DORNEY SCHOOL

This came about as a result of Foster's Education Act of 1870, the original building costing £750 and accommodating one Certified teacher and 75 children. Most long serving and celebrated head teacher was Eleanor Catherine Bennett who came from Gloucestershire in 1919, her fiancé having been killed in the Great War. She served the school with energy and dignity until her retirement in 1952. It's now Dorney County Combined School, 87% of pupils achieving Level 4 results in Key Stage Two English, Maths and Science.

Eton

Kelly's 1956 Directory of Windsor and neighbourhood tells us "Eton has long been celebrated for its great college, which has maintained its pre-eminence amongst the public schools of England, since its foundation by Henry VI, October 11th 1440. An annual inclusive fee of £45 is charged for the education and maintenance of each scholar."

KNOWING YOUR PLACE

We were told of the '10 and three 30s' road to success: 10% is applied intelligence, 30% is access to resources, 30% is high self-esteem, and 30% is a public school accent. During our five month journey we've occasionally encountered evidence that would suggest there could be some truth in this.

SLOUGH HEAT AND POWER

An environmentally-friendly plant on the Slough Trading Estate, umbilically connected to the Mars bar factory, to which they supply electricity and steam. Why steam, Uncle Mike? To keep melted chocolate moving through pipes. They burn fibre fuel from packaging waste and chipped wood supplied by tree surgeons. What's umbilical? Ask your mother.

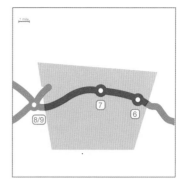

COPTHORNE

Legoland gave them a dragon – the size of an Alsatian and very heavy, but someone nicked it. Then a Welsh man left his car behind, unlocked, with the log book inside. And it's still here, six months later, despite their phone calls to him.

ASDA

They do the biggest off-the-hanger bras, according to Bristol's enhanced glamour model Cathy Barry.

COURTYARD

When there was a very small fire on the 9th floor, receptionist Kelly Smith evacuated the building, then ran up all the stairs with the fire brigade, but realised she'd forgotten the pass key, so ran down again and back up, so the boys could blow out a very small flame.

TOWER AND ASHBOURNE

These are down the road from the Slough Family Centre, which provides assessments for children in need and organises fostering care for Slough council.

SLOUGH SEWAGE WORKS

"Warning. This is a water company operation site and as such contains areas of deep or fast flowing water together with machinery and structures which may be hazardous to the unwary."

SLOUGH-WINDSOR

Eton College was strongly opposed to the Paddington-Maidenhead Railway Line. The GWR bill of 1835 stated that no branch line to Windsor would be laid and that no station would be built within three miles of the college.

JUBILEE RIVER

It's that artificial river again, which didn't live up to expectations. Floods hit Datchet in 2003, and so the Environment Agency are spending £1.3 million to improve the banks of the Myrke Ditch.

Windsor

'The Queen's Castle' on BBC1 didn't make it clear that the Royal Family have an unrivalled view of the Mars bar factory, and can get takeaways literally across the road from Burger King, McDonalds and Pizza Hut.

It costs £12.50 to enter the Castle, and they ask you to fill in one of those forms if you are a UK taxpayer to claim some of it back from the Exchequer.

The place is enormous. Nearly as big as the Wilkinson depot at Newport.

If you're going to do the Royal thing, we recommend their Farm Shop down the other end of the Home Park. Free parking, excellent produce and good café.

In case you think a Royal Borough is immune from the problems we've seen in every local newspaper, it's recent Newsletter front page story is about the council's determination "to vanquish vandalism, conquer car crime, eliminate litter, banish binge drinking and get rid of graffiti."

We're sending the Queen a copy of this, as she commutes to Buckingham Palace along our carriageway. Then we might become Motorway Sights Guide suppliers by Royal Appointment. Okay, maybe not.

KEY WEST

Newsweek magazine and Misys computer software are the major tenants here. It's the side of the building we can see from the M4. Next to it on the main road is Edinburgh House, which is across the road from a new office block with a circular tower on top: Charter Court – only visible to us when the traffic's crawling. As we pass, let's remember Slough gave Britain the Aspro, Bakelite, Horlicks and ICI Paint, to name but a few.

ST MARYS, SLOUGH

The construction of this "cathedral-proportioned" building occupied John Oldrid Scott (son of Sir Gilbert) from 1875 til his death in 1913, with the completion of the 50 metre spire. Almost 300 names on the Great War memorial outside the front door. Around the base is the inscription: "Who stands if freedom falls? Who dies if England live? There is but one task for all. One life for each to give."

PATRIOT COURT

Built in 1978 and recently re-furbished to accommodate Amazon, the internet book vendors.▲

NEW CENTURY HOUSE (W.O.)

A new block offering 64,000 square feet of office space.

RIDING COURT FARM

Behind this shed are a series of barn conversion offices, one home to the Pampered Chef, the UK base of an outfit that sells kitchen tools through home demonstrations. Worldwide there are 70,000 Kitchen Consultants preparing meals and selling utensils in the culinary and commercial footsteps of founder Doris Christopher.

2358   2340

2361   2354   2350

Slough

You've landed on Planet Mars where the natives harvest the bars day and night and ship them out into every possible space on earth.

Many of Britain's most important and influential post-war businesses were, and, in some cases, still are, based here, often occupying distinctive, dedicated premises on the A4. Visit Slough Museum and invest in the STEAM (Slough Town Employment Action Movement) histories for full details.

The Road Research Laboratory used the town in the 1950s as a guinea pig for a whole variety of traffic manipulation and control measures that would subsequently be applied nationally.

The Slough unitary authority was one of six created when the County Council of Berkshire was broken up in 1998.

We were assured that no manager in the public or private sector bears any resemblance whatsoever to Ricky Gervais's David Brent character from 'The Office'.

GAWPABILITY

You're now passing Datchet, that lies on the route of the Windsor Castle open-topped tour buses. The guides must have plenty of patter to see them through here, as there are two railway level crossings which frequently halt all traffic. Doubtless they mention the curious fact that a pub in this well-appointed village has been named after the communist newspaper, the Morning Star.

Legoland

Some leaflets claim the Madejski Hotel in Reading is an "ideal base to visit Legoland... 20 minutes drive away." Well, the land of Lego is just south of Windsor on the A3022, 15 miles away as the crow flies and 20 miles by road from the football ground. We can't see how you could get there in 20 minutes without picking up speeding tickets.

ST MARY THE VIRGIN, DATCHET

First built in 1350 to advance the influence of the Order of the Garter, there's a memorial to Christopher Barker, printer to Queen Elizabeth the First, inside. Later, of course, came Her Majesty's Stationery Office.

SATELLITE SPOTTING

Ditton Park, once the home of Lady Montague, was the Radio Research Station for many years, engineers working out of coke stove-heated wooden sheds, with experimental antennae frequently knocked over by cows in the fields. In the 1960s it became the Radio and Space Research Station and started spotting Russian Sputniks.

MARRIOTT

As a handy base for the Windsor dog show, they allow guests to bring their dogs in. One morning a maid went into a guest's empty room and turned back the duvet to discover a python. Best guest so far: Jennifer Aniston, who was filming down the road at Pinewood.

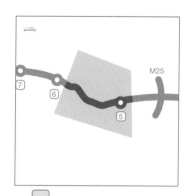

COMPUTER ASSOCIATES

The world's fourth largest software company has its European, Middle East and Africa headquarters here in the grounds of Ditton Manor Park. 800 people produce business IT software.

JAMES MEADOW

A shared ownership Housing Association block at the front of the Langley Woods estate. The private houses behind start at quarter-of-a-million.

POPLAR HOUSE

Dew Pitchmastic branded their scaffolding with colour netting whilst doing up this place for Slough council in 2005.

BYRON & LINDEN

The Housing Corporation has refurbished these 120 flats "to improve the quality of life for local people". Behind them Brockway and Albion are soon to be replaced with low level properties.

2330

J5

QUEEN MOTHER RESERVOIR

We can see the bank of this massive structure that is more than a mile long and just one of seven similar huge reservoirs holding most the water required by west London. In surface area they take up about the same space as the Heathrow site. Apparently demand is close to exceeding supply.

HONDA HQ

700 franchised businesses in the UK are monitored from here. Their Civic 1.3 IMA Executive came out top in the Environmental Transport Association's rankings. It runs on petrol but engages an electric motor when accelerating. Then going downhill the battery gets recharged, hence Integrated Motor Assist.

Ascot Racecourse

Lord Hinchingbrook was Steward in 1788, and set some new standards, including: "no person do bring dogs on the course, as there will be proper persons appointed to destroy them."

Down the road is an exclusive golf club where Prince Andrew used to turn up and flout the etiquette, much to the annoyance of the regulars. The Club Secretary was in despair until one of the committee members said he'd have a word with the boy's mother, we were told by someone who knows.

Langley

Hawker Siddley built an aircraft factory here in the 1930s, and by 1942 was turning out five Hawker Hurricanes each day. After the war, London County Council established a huge housing estate in the district, and the aircraft works became a Ford truck factory, delivering the Transit van from 1965. In 1986 Fiat took over the business and turned out Ford Iveco trucks until the plant closed in 1997 with 450 job losses.

M25

"The orbital motorway is a security collar fixed to the neck of a convicted criminal. It enforces a nocturnal quarantine." "The M25, from being the pet and pride of an autocratic government, has been rapidly downgraded to a rage-inducing asteroid belt, debris bumping and farting and belching around a sealed-off city," reckons Iain Sinclair in his 'London Orbital' book, that's considered the bee's knees in some circles.

On the few dozen occasions we've used the M25, it's functioned just fine.

Sinclair slumped round the corridor on foot, John Walsh of the Independent declaring him a genius. You can buy the hardback from Granta for £25. Now that is clever. The M25 for 25 quid.

Watford

"It has been suggested that the 'Wat' may have been a person, or may have simply meant 'wet', explains Roy Phippen in his pretty little new 'Travelling the M25 Clockwise.' It's big on aerial snaps and cute design, but gives short shrift to the fascinating de Havilland museum near South Mimms. We hear Roy's going to tackle the M1. Cheeky bastard. Didn't he know we were going to do that! Wonder if he'll give our M6 Guide a mention when he gets to Rugby?

GALILEO

All those IT systems that allow travel agents to integrate airline flights, hotel accommodation, car hire and what have you are managed from here. And it's where e-bookers come down to earth.

ROYAL MAIL

This is their state-of-the-art Heathrow Worldwide Distribution Centre, sorting and X-raying up to 40,000 international parcels an hour.

BRIDGESTONE

As well as ones for ordinary cars, they do motor racing tyres, and round the other side of Heathrow they do great big ones for aeroplanes.

COLNE BROOK

Splits from the River Colne up at Uxbridge and reaches the Thames 4 miles south of here at Runnymede.

CAR SPARES

The West Drayton "big breakers" have been here for 50 years, long before either motorway came along. "Come in, say what you want, slip us a drink, and we'll get it for you." But don't turn up at five to five on a Friday when they're getting their wage slips.

J4b

Colnbrook

Once a tiny coaching community on the Great Bath Road, this village is now merely a mile from the forthcoming Terminal 5, so the sweet old Ostrich Hotel (dating from 1106, and claiming King John popped in for refreshments on his way to sign the Magna Carta at Runnymede in 1215) may soon become a McDonalds, the rest of the main street a Holiday Inn, and all gardens and surrounding fields will be tarmacked over for valet parking.

LONDON CONCRETE

This is the most productive concrete processing plant in Europe, and it's in the top ten in the whole world, operating 24 hours a day, 7 days a week.

YEWSLEY-POYNE

Delivers sand from Colchester and hard stone from the Mendips for London Concrete.

RIVER COLNE

South of here it passes British Airways Waterside offices and Harmondsworth Moor, "the largest public park to be built in the London area in the last 100 years." Who paid for it? BA (profits in 2005: £415m). "Ancient meadows have been created using specially harvested seed."

ST MARY'S, HARMONDSWORTH

It's across the road from Harmondsworth Hall guest house, that's a hugely pleasant contrast to the uniformity of most Heathrow hotels, and is handy for the excellent Sipson Tandoori. Of course Harmondsworth is where Penguin books used to come from. ▶

COLNBROOK WASTE REDUCTION CENTRE

Grundon operate this site. Recycle for London say: Reuse things, Think about what you buy, Buy recycled products and Compost food and garden waste.

CROWNE PLAZA

Opened by Sarah, Duchess of York, in 1998. They've had Phil Collins, Cliff Richard, Tony Bennett, Howard Keele, Jack Jones, Warren Beatty, Robert Plant, Robert Maxwell ("horrible man") the Rev. Ian Paisley and Kylie Minogue stay here. And someone once left behind a false leg.

NOVOTEL

Heathrow hang-out for Malev flight crew, who are bigger than you think, with twenty 737s and a couple of Fokkers, according to a plane spotter at the Visitor Centre. Let's hope those Hungarians go easy on the Prague Staropramen lager on tap, which caused us to lose our raison d'etre after half a pint.

Hayes

The 1868 National Gazetteer of Great Britain explained that, at Lady Dacre's bequest, there is "a presentation of two aged persons of either sex to Emanuel Hospital, Westminster. There are National Schools for both sexes; also a lunatic asylum for the middle and upper classes."

PREMIER TRAVEL LODGE

On a Hotel Breaks website we booked a Heathrow Premier Travel Lodge. The site offered a map that we printed out and tried to use to find the place, but the map was wrong. We phoned Hotel Breaks to alert them to the error and were told all complaints have to be in writing.

HAYES FIRE STATION

This is a standard issue Middlesex design of station, occupying a busy patch.

Four watches of 15 men can take three appliances (a pump, pump ladder and aerial ladder platform) to attend to incidents on the M4 and M25, as well as at Heathrow and at Northolt military airfield. Over a typical 2 day/2 night tour they deal with 45 calls.

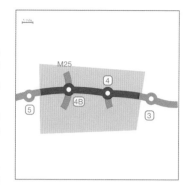

COMFORT INN

There are 5,000 hotel bedrooms around Heathrow. This one's particularly close to the "haaarsh" noise, but may be relieved of that in due course if plans are pursued to put this stretch of the M4 inside a tunnel fitted with scrubbers to remove nitrogen dioxide emissions from vehicle fumes to make environmentally acceptable the anticipated increased traffic for the airport.

HOLIDAY INN

Was it a good idea to build this massive 608-room structure here, when nothing else goes above 5 storeys? If you open the window at the end of the corridor on the ninth floor north wing you get a bird's eye view of the work going on for the development of Terminal 5.

ST PETERS, HARLINGTON

At the other end of the road is the Heathrow Therapy Centre: psychology and hypnotherapy for stress, phobias, obsessions and compulsions.

HARLINGTON GRAVEL PIT

A market gardener provided Covent Garden with veg from these fields until he retired at the age of 90. Now local firm Streeter extract high quality sand and ballast from here, and from a similar plant closer to Junction 4.

Heathrow

The world's biggest airport began life as the Great West Aerodrome in the 1930s. Now the site covers more than 3 square miles, on which 1,250 aircraft land or leave each day, carrying between them nearly 200,000 passengers and 3,000 tonnes of cargo. 80 airlines take people to and from 180 destinations with New York, Dublin, Paris, Amsterdam, Edinburgh and Glasgow most popular, two-thirds of the journeys being leisure rather than business. It provides work for 70,000, including 3,000 baggage handlers, over 1,000 security staff and 800 aircraft cleaners.

The NCP Terminal 1A Short Stay car park costs £2.20 for 30 minutes, through to £86 for 48 hours, after which it's £43 per day. We were told it's not uncommon for vehicles to remain there for 4 months or more.

Inexplicably, the Government is allowing BAA to open a Fifth Terminal, to increase passenger numbers from 60 million to 90 million per annum. It's going up apace alongside the A3044 and will have a dedicated link off the M25.

The Secretary of the Harmondsworth Residents Association reckons it's a violation of Human Rights.

NESTLES

This is where coffee comes from. Well, Nescafe. Since 1938, they've been turning out instant coffee at this Hayes factory, once the concept of applying boiling water to granules was perfected by Swiss scientist Max Mortgenthaler.

SOUTHALL GAS TANK

Southall Gas was absorbed by the Brentford Gas Company, which was taken over by Gas, Light and Coke in 1926. This became the North Thames Gas Board in 1949, and now what's left is Transco Site 960.

1 – 16 MOSTON CLOSE

These flats are in Cranford Park, which was owned in the 17th century by Sir Roger Aston, Keeper of the Great Wardrobe, Barber and Gentleman of the Bedchamber to King James the First.

TNT

"All goods are carried subject to our Conditions of Carriage which are available on request. It is in your interest to read them as your rights may be affected."

NEVILL LONG

He does suspended ceilings, partition-ing and plasterboard systems.

LOWERY

HQ of a 50 year old firm that provides construction services to the rail, power and telecommunications industries.

HESTON EAST

Why would anyone want services here? Well, you might be desperate for a toilet, or need an A to Z. There's a Congestion Charge ticket dispenser, with 42 buttons on it (admittedly including all letters of the alphabet). It'll take you 10 minutes just to read the instructions – a serious challenge for newcomers.

ST DUNSTANS, CRANFORD PARK

Buried here in 1856 was John Finall Cook, the "worst used" High Constable of Hounslow Heath for over 50 years.

The Gloucestershire Berkeley family spent summers in the adjoining manor house for three centuries. It was demolished in 1945, but there's a manned information centre where we watched a TV camera feed of 6 day old blue tits being fed caterpillars by their parents.

RIVER CRANE

Southward, it skirts round Hounslow before reaching the Thames, passing the site of an old gunpowder factory, then Hounslow military barracks, established after the English Civil War to keep loyal soldiers handy for the City.

Feltham

Home of DHL, Welcome Car Finance, the Hounslow Urban Farm and the St Giles Hotel, cleverly converted from an old British Rail office building. To clarify, only the hotel occupies the old BR building; the others have their own premises.

HESTON MAINTENANCE DEPOT

Jobs as Highways Agency Traffic Officers going here. "You will have wide-ranging powers, allowing you to stop and divert traffic, close roads and lanes and operate traffic signs and remove vehicles – only the most responsible and reliable need apply." £16,171 + up to 20% shift allowance + £1,000.

HESTON WEST

Why would anyone want services here? Well, you might have realised you've not got enough petrol, or you need a road map of Britain. BT stuck a 'Business Centre' in here, but it hasn't hugely caught on, as businessmen and women all have to arrive from one direction and later all leave in one direction.

Staines

"I can help you solve all your worries and matters regarding bringing back loved ones, breaking all sorts of black magic, bad luck, career, business, court cases, exams, family problems, sexual difficulties, depression, addiction, anti-social behaviour, job, and so many other things", declares Sheikh Sanou in the Staines Guardian What's On pages, but the man himself is actually on the Great West Road in Hounslow.

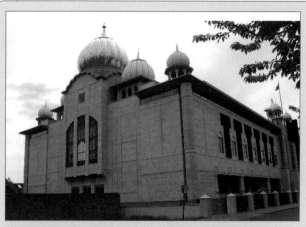

GURDWARA SRI GURU SINGH SABHA, SOUTHALL (W.O.)

Built at a cost of £17.5 million, all raised from public subscription, this Sikh Temple, opened in March 2003, is the largest in Europe. We walked in off the street and were greeted warmly. If you remove your shoes, have a wash and cover your head, you can enjoy free vegetarian food prepared by volunteers in the langer hall from 3.30 am until 9 pm each day. Prince Charles, Michael Howard and the Archbishop of Canterbury have tried it and liked it. 30,000 visit each week. All religions welcome, if they respect the strict ban on alcohol.

ST THOMAS THE APOSTLE, HANWELL (E.O.)

It's just up the road from Elthorne Park Sports Centre and High School, which has had a "Green Corridor" funded wildlife garden since 2000, in which pupils have spotted 40 types of birds and 8 types of butterflies.

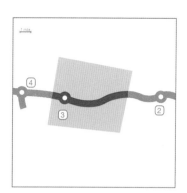

GRAND UNION CANAL/RIVER BRENT

This canal was one of the key arteries connecting the Midlands to London. Just north of here it conjoins with the River Brent, which comes from Barnet through – you've got it - Brent Cross, then Ealing, Perivale and, yes, Brent Valley Golf Courses, before spilling into the Thames at – why, Brentford, of course, just south of here.

OUR LADY, QUEEN OF THE APOSTLES, HESTON

A heart-warming atmosphere at the Sunday morning Pentecost Mass, with lots of smart looking worshippers happily arriving on foot, in the sun, to the sound of a pretty peal of bells. It touched us and made us think that the cross on top of that needle must be an effective conduit for the goodness of God reaching this place and its people.

HESTON FARM

Fenton and Bellamy House dominate the estate. We noticed a roll of carpet perched perilously on a 5th floor balcony and so phoned Hounslow Homes who cheerfully said they'd check it out. Their mission statement: to deliver excellent housing services and encourage the development of sustainable local communities. The team can speak Punjabi, Hindi, Gujarati and Swahili.

OSTERLEY PARK

The ivy-covered walled garden lies at the edge of this National Trust property that the Chief Executive of West London Business, Frank Wingate, reckons passengers waiting to change planes at Heathrow could pop out to for a quick visit. West London wants a bigger portion of the tourist dollar, according to the Brentford, Chiswick and Isleworth Times.

SOUTHALL-BRENTFORD EAST

Constructed by Brunel to take GWR goods to Brentford Docks. Now it delivers aggregates to London Concrete and takes away 66 containers of household rubbish to a landfill site in Oxfordshire every evening.

WYKE GREEN GOLF CLUB

18 holes 6211 yards. Green Fees: Monday to Thursday £30 per day, £18 after 3.30pm. Visitor policy: Welcome with Handicap Certificate weekdays; weekends only with a member until after 4pm. How the hell would you get your golf clubs here, you're thinking. Well, believe it or not, after 9.30 in the morning, the traffic's not too bad.

Uxbridge

Harry Inglis's 1950s Contour Road Books of England were designed to alert motorists of challenging gradients, where "the loss of momentum on the ascent makes the last part of the climb a more severe task for the engine." Addressing this place, he warns that the tram lines from Ealing reach here, but "after Uxbridge the road has good surface and is well engineered, with gradients seldom above 1 in 21 to High Wycombe."

Harrow

For people who think today's schools are under-resourced, consider that when the establishment here opened in the 16th century, parents were obliged to provide their male offspring with their own books, paper, pens, ink, candles, and bows and arrows.

SECRET STUFF

Readers may be surprised to know that we are minded to respect Government guidelines as publishers and so not draw attention to certain institutions and facilities that lie at certain points in the vicinity of the M4 corridor.

WEMBLEY ON ITS WAY?

We reached here in the month of May, when leaves were abundant on trees and shrubs, so from our excellent Rover 45 we couldn't tell if the new arch at the football stadium would be visible in winter. You can certainly see it from footbridges. Come November, check it out.

BOSTON MANOR-OSTERLEY

This is the Heathrow arm of the Piccadilly line. The first length of the London Underground opened in 1863. Now they've got 253 miles of route with 275 stations. And every weekday 5 million passenger journeys are made.

LONDON PLAYING FIELDS

Providing cricket in the summer and rugby pitches in the winter, serviced by a lonely pavilion sitting under the carriageway, these are privately run playing fields, right next to Hounslow Council's Boston Manor Park.

HOLLOWAYS

They've been hand-sorting non-ferrous metals since 1892. Gary Holloway values friendliness, fair prices and fast turn around.

EXPRESS ASPHALT

"Warning, if amber light comes on, proceed with caution. If red light comes on and klaxon sounds, stop pumping immediately."

SPACE STATION

Britain's oldest self storage firm and founder member of the UK Self Storage Association, representing Brentford, West London, Slough and Berkshire.

LONDON CONCRETE

"Report to plant manager prior to discharging. Maximum blow pressure 10 psi. Maximum blow temperature 60 C. Please remain with vehicle whilst discharging."

DAY AGGREGATES

"Please observe the following whilst in the depot. Safely helmets, safety footwear and high visibility clothing to be worn on site. Give way to loading shovels and trains at all times."

WEST WASTE

Transfer station for the West London Waste Authority, contracted to manage recycling for Brent, Ealing, Harrow, Hillingdon, Hounslow and Richmond. That's a lot of rubbish. Who said: Just like the rest of this book?

GILLETTE

"Shave Test Office requires intelligent junior interested in figures and graphs. Age 15/17. Gillette Safety Razor Company." Situations Vacant column of the Brentford and Chiswick Times of March 1965. Maybe the person who got that job is still in these stylish premises on the Great West Road.

CAPITAL CITY

Yeah, we know you've seen many signs along the last 100 miles telling you how far you are away from London, but we would not be so presumptuous to include an entry explaining something about this place to newcomers, or digging out old tourist guide entries.

Instead we will simply observe that most of it seems to us a great place, full of character, charm and busyness. We've worked in Soho, St John's Wood and Shepherds Bush, and never fail to be engaged by the people, buildings and services, almost of all of which function superbly well despite the constant pressures of space, time and competition. We recommend you walk as much as possible, which is a never-ending, richly-textured joy. Second choice is the bus, from where you can relish a cross-section of humanity and urban landscapes for hours on end for a couple of pounds. To complete our journey eastward from west Wales, we got the bus from Chiswick to Hyde Park, then walked along Piccadilly to the Circus in order to do the fundamental tourist thing of sitting on the steps below Eros, which we'd never tried before. An immensely pleasant free hour in a fantastic city.

North & South Circular

Chiswick Flyover defines the western joint of the London ring roads. Going north - which we don't recommend if you can avoid it - you head through Ealing, Stonebridge, Neasden, the start of the M1, East Finchley, New Southgate, Edmonton, South Chingford, Walthamstow, South Woodford, Wanstead, and Beckton, where-upon you arrive at the London City Airport and the Woolwich Ferry across the Thames.

From Chiswick the South Circular finds a tortuous way through North and East Sheen, Roehampton, Wandsworth, Clapham, Streatham, Tulse Hill, Dulwich, Forest Hill, Catford, Hither Green and Woolwich, to reach the south side of the ferry.

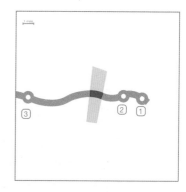

MORNING CAMPUS

The Berkeley Group are in the process of constructing a huge new facility for Thames Valley University. A 17 storey block will house nearly 900 student study bedrooms here. There will be provision for 220 key workers and 9,000 square metres of "academic floor space", which is what used to be called classrooms. When they're finished we'll be looking at the tallest structure along the M4. You'll be able to draw a little picture of it across this text.

GLAXOSMITHKLINE

Britain's biggest drug firm since SmithKline Beecham merged with Glaxo Wellcome in 2000. Seldom out of the business press for big profits, big board room salaries, big legal issues and big investment risks. We were indifferent to their fortunes until realising these were the people who had created Ventolin, puffs of which have brought merciful relief from asthmatic misery to millions, including us. A big thank you.

1000

Many motorists will remember this as Wang House, which is how it's still designated in the Collins London Street Atlas. Well, Wang's long gone, we don't know where. For a while an outfit called Comdisco dominated a couple of floors. Now, amongst others, we find Sword, IT consultants "focused on creating a structured and compatible environment for financial profitability and personal satisfaction."

PROFILE WEST (E.O.)

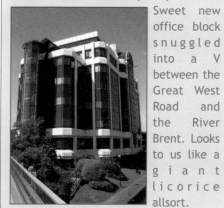

Sweet new office block snuggled into a V between the Great West Road and the River Brent. Looks to us like a giant licorice allsort.

GREAT WEST & COMPUTER HOUSE

These have been here since before the M4. The big one's Great West, occupied by Air India and Star Advertising, whilst in Computer House we find IT managers Steria and a leg of Allianz Cornhill: Petplan, the world's largest provider of pet insurance, who have so far paid out £30 million world-wide as a result of animal accidents.

OUR LADY & ST JOHN'S SCHOOL

This Catholic Nursery and Primary School draws in around 250 kids aged between 3 and 11, mostly from within the Parish of St John's. The nice new circular building has been here for about 14 years. When we spoke to them they were not at all phased by the prospect of the looming tower of the Thames Valley University campus that will grow up alongside.

CASUALTY PLUS

See a doctor for just £39. Health screens range from £49 to £349 (that would be quite a lot of screening). They also do laboratory tests, occupational health, physiotherapy, a travel clinic and X-rays. It's step-off-the-street private medicine, available from 8 in the morning til 8 at night, 8 days a week – sorry, 7 days a week.

ST JOHNS, BRENTFORD

This was a chapel in the grounds of Boston Manor House which lies half a mile to the north, and, in the 17th century, was the home of Sir Edward Spencer, an ancestor of Diana, Princess of Wales.

GLOBE

A classic London pub. We called in on Saturday night when Terry Donovan's Blues Band were doing a set, and pretty barmaids were serving Fullers London Pride, delivered from the Lamb Brewery just beyond the end of the motorway on the A4 at the Hogarth roundabout.

EXION (W.O.)

There used to be a Baptist Church here. Now it's a speculatively built office block designed as smart headquarters for a firm that might have good reasons for wanting to be close to GlaxoSmith Kline. If you've got a java-enabled browser you can take an ehouse tour.

VAN WAGNER

State of the art advertising unit, below which is a cluster of satellite dishes bouncing Reuter news in and out of the UK.
Yes, that's what it's like underneath the M4.

26 GLENHURST ROAD

This was once a Registry Office, then it became the base for Hounslow's Environmental drainage and community team, some of whom had got married here. It's now been sold to the private sector and may become a hotel or more likely apartments.

Hounslow

This is a formidable slice of the London pie stretching along the north bank of the Thames from Chiswick to south of Heathrow. It was first coaching stop on the Great West Road and so had stabling for 1,000 horses back in 1800. In WW2 dozens of Hounslow citizens were killed by German flying bombs. As well as the obvious stuff you'd expect of a London borough, they're big on biodiversity, green walking routes (superbly illustrated with a set of aerial photos of their six major parks) and 30 allotments sites (where slow worms nest in compost heaps). They provide a housebound library service and operate a Late Night Noise Team.

LONDON TRANSPORT

Phenomenally effective in our view; for example: Wimbledon railway station has nine platforms, and Platform Five is long enough to take an eight-carriage train, such as the 7.45 am for Clapham Junction and Victoria. Each carriage has 72 seats and they're all occupied, with more people standing, so there are around 90 in each carriage as the train comes to a halt at 7.45 am. When the doors open, about 40 people disembark and about 200 cram in, all in about 30 seconds. The train is stationary at the platform for less than a minute. Guess how long until the next Clapham/Victoria train arrives? Three minutes later. Yes, we kid you not. This is the pitch of morning commuter passenger processing.

We salute Transport for London for sustaining this service so effectively and efficiently, albeit seriously short of space and comfort. Us hicks from the sticks are humbled by this facility, capacity, mass movement of humanity, with seldom a hiccup.

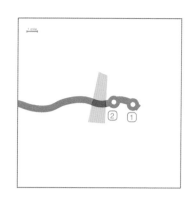

TOYOTA

You can buy a Prius petrol-electric hybrid car at Currie Motors. The Prius has been chosen by the Environment Agency as their fleet vehicle for those staff who have to drive round town. It got the lowest score in the Agency's evaluation of exhaust emissions and is exempt from London congestion charges.

GET OUT OF YOUR CARS

With the exception of London, 75% of daily commuting is done by car, generating the highest carbon dioxide emissions per passenger journey on land. It is estimated that commuting motorists in some British cities will have spent approximately six months of their lives stuck in a traffic jam if things carry on the way they are. Satellite-controlled road pricing may inhibit some journeys for those with low levels of disposable income, freeing up the carriageway for rich people in their big fuel and fume heavy vehicles. In 'How we can save the planet' Mayer Hillman points out that calculating personal carbon dioxide emissions is essential to increase individual and collective awareness of our responsibility for climate change. He believes every individual should be given equal allocations of energy vouchers.

DOME SERVICE STATION

Texaco are not allowed to put advertising on the top of the triangular brick column, which is a poor substitute for the earlier stylish Lex Dome art deco structure designed to draw motorists in for fuel. The busy service station below still trades as the Dome. At the bottom of the brick stalk is an old BT pay phone.

NEW ENGLAND

It's more like a disco inside than a pub. The landlady is very hopeful that the re-development of the laboratories next door will bring fresh custom. She used to do loads of Beecham business lunches every day, and things have never been the same since.

NEW CENTRE?

Hopes are high that this old Alfa Laval building will become affordable housing, courtesy of Hounslow Council.

WESTGATE HOUSE

Soon to be demolished, to make way for new homes and offices.

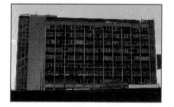

BRENTFORD TOWERS

East to west are Wickstead, Fraser, Cornish, Harvey, Maudsley and Boulton House, of which we've pictured the last two. If you're new to landing planes at Heathrow, just remember to keep these giant markers on your right, then look out for the Holiday Inn ahead, and the runway's just south of that.

GRIFFIN PARK

Brentford FC manager Martin Allen thought the boys could do with a rest back in March, so he fixed for them to fly from Heathrow to the Gulf for a few days, but got the flight time wrong and discovered they needed to be at the airport just a few hours after playing Colchester at Colchester. The Bees won the game and got the plane.

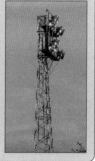

LOOKING UP, LOOKING DOWN

The neat solution to routing the motorway out of Chiswick was to build it above the existing Great West Road. So you're travelling on a platform that lies across a line of concrete and steel stalks that form a central reservation for the A4 below. We walked along the A4, beneath the M4 for a couple of miles, to get our pictures, and next day Catherine Taylor, local history specialist at Chiswick Library, showed us aerial photos taken during the construction period, underpinning our appreciation of the clever civil engineering that has served us all superbly well for 40 years.

MERCEDES, BRENTFORD

You can occasionally pick up an early E200 for just £5,000 (though perhaps not from this forecourt). "Over-engineered tank-like indulgence, with an interior like a Dutch brothel", according to Used Car Buyer magazine.

Next door was the 'Lucozade Annexe' that had a big animated "Replaces lost energy" neon sign on the side. The Twentieth Century Society mounted an empassioned bid to keep it up, but failed.

CARVILLE HALL PARK

The patches of greenery either side of the curious but effective set of ramps on and off the M4 that constitute Junction 2 are the two halves of a park that have Hounslow Council managed football pitches on the north side and an attractive 19th century villa split into apartments on the south side. And you thought this might have been a handy multi-storey.

PARK VIEW

Parsons E&C design facilities for Shell and BP oil and gas operations. E and C stand for energy and chemicals. The company will soon be known as Worley Parsons due to a tie up with Australia. They were in the Data General building next door but moved into this place when it opened a couple of years ago. The Park of which they have a view is Gunnersbury, round the back.

WALLIS HOUSE

Back in the Sixties, the letters B E E C H A M were grandly displayed along the top of one side, and L U C O Z A D E on the other, because this was HQ of the pharmaceutical group before they moved up the road.

Of course, in those days a Beechams powder and a glass of Lucozade would cure more or less anything. Thomas Wallis designed the Hoover building and other 1930s workplaces. Barratts hope to turn this into apartments.

27 GREAT WEST ROAD

The three big occupants platform their logos on the sides. Sega, Agfa and Whatman.

We know what the first two do (yes, electronic games and photography), but who's Whatman? He was a paper maker whose legacy is now sophisticated filtering media to separate chemical components for everything from foodstuffs to DNA.

REGATTA POINT

An office building now done up as fancy flats. "From the motorway you can see the unattractive Northern side." It's got "manicured lawns" and an on-site concierge.

KEW BRIDGE STEAM MUSEUM

They've got the largest working beam engine in the world in here, where five Cornish engines used to pump West London's water supply. It's now an Engineering Heritage Hallmark site.

EMC2

Stands for Enterprise Content Management Two. In what was the Data General building they do information systems for business. "An integrated set of content, process and repository technologies." The look of the building reflects the shape of the clock next door, which EMC2 have branded their own.

EMC2 CLOCK

It's been here since before the M4 elevated carriageway was erected and used to have Martini logos on its sides. At the base are local offices of the Shaw Trust, who provide training and work opportunities for people who are disadvantaged in the labour market due to disability or ill health.

VANTAGE WEST

This building's been on the Great West Road since the early 1960s. CGG stands for Compagnie Generale De Geophysique. They do sophisticated surveying of the earth's surface, not least for the oil and gas industries. They've got land-based and sea-based teams and equipment to acquire data on the nature of rock and sea-bed environments.

GUNNERSBURY CEMETERY

Contains the Katyn Memorial to the thousands of Poles who were "murdered by the Soviet secret police on Stalin's orders in 1940, as finally admitted in April 1990 by the USSR after 50 years shameful denial of the truth." 14,500 Polish soldiers went missing and the remains of 4,500 were uncovered at Katyn. When we visited, 8 petrol-driven strimmers were buzzing through the foliage, like a swarm of giant wasps.

SOTHEBYS

The antique dealers' warehouses are here, receiving and delivering expensive old objects, not just within the UK but overseas too.

DHL

This is a training centre. Let's hope they don't practice on anything belonging to their neighbours.

RIVERS HOUSE

This is older than it looks - one of a number of sixties buildings round here that has been given a major facelift, inside and out. The fancy apartments are above Kew Bridge tube station, and just 5 minutes walk from Kew Gardens.

SOUTH ACTION–BRENTFORD/KEW BRIDGE

We're passing over a busy little bit of the 788 kilometres of overground rail lines within the Greater London Transport network.

CAPITAL COURT

This is Waterstone's Head Office, from where they manage their 150 odd branches. Gardners, the Eastbourne-based book distributors, supply Waterstone's bookshops all over the country with copies of our Guides (which always do best when there's a pile near the counter).

THE BIG GREEN PARCEL MACHINE

has a depot in this long silver and red shed. It's Tuffnells, begun in Sheffield by Harold Tuffnell in the 1920s with a horse and cart, and now utilising 25 depots across the UK.

CITROEN

The London West dealership is indebted to Andre Citroen who first made cars in his own name in 1919, and soon hit on chevron-shaped gear teeth, which resulted in the double chevron emblem on this marque.

Chiswick

A lovely place, extremely well documented by Gillian Clegg, who, in her next edition will have to update the sweet old Italian Foubert's Hotel entry, that Ant and Dec are threatening to turn into a glitzy nightclub. Industrial heritage? Thorneycroft steam launches on the Thames, Cherry Blossom shoe polish and Sanderson wallpaper. Past celeb residents? Eamonn Andrews, Tommy Cooper and Donald Pleasance. Eat at Silk and Spice, 95 High Road.

B&Q

Big on sponsoring round the globe boating.

LION USED CARS

"Peugeot Citroen's industrial sites do not rank among the biggest energy consumers. A number of vehicle production processes nevertheless consume significant amounts of energy, particularly casting, drying, paint baking, heat treatment and heating. The Group's total energy consumption is equal to 1.5% of the energy consumed by industry in France."

BSI

This building was erected as the UK HQ of IBM, when their state-of-the-art 360 computer took up an air-conditioned, temperature-controlled room the size of a restaurant and couldn't do much more than a modern mobile phone.
Now it's HQ of the British Standards Institute.

CATHEDRAL OF THE DORMITION OF THE MOST HOLY MOTHER OF GOD AND THE HOLY ROYAL MARTYRS

This is the most important of half a dozen Russian Orthodox Churches in the U.K. A sign in the porch reads: "No women wearing trousers in this church please."

J1

TIE RACK

As well as occupying 3 Great West Road (architects Norman Levinson and partners, 1984) they've got some warehousing round the back stuffed full of Italian Frangi fashion as well as neckwear.

BRENTFORD FOUNTAIN LEISURE CENTRE

This well-appointed facility, with a super swimming pool, was opened by the Rt Hon Neil Kinnock on 28th July 1987. In school holidays, kids can attend the Sports Camp while Mums do Cardio Sculpt.

WHEATSTONE HOUSE

Chiswick roundabout used to be almost in the country, with a little Esso petrol kiosk on one corner, when this flagship office complex went up next to it in 1953, making it by far the biggest building in the area. Now it's a Customer Management Centre for BT's Conferencing Services. Wheatstone invented perforated tape for telegraphy in 1867.

JUNCTION 1

Originally ramps ran from the roundabout on to the elevated section to the west, but now Junction 1 is not really a junction at all, as you can't get on or off the M4 here. The A4 simply becomes the M4 as it rises from road level.

HEADING OUT OF TOWN?

So you're going to use the book starting from the back to reveal the contents as you move west. In theory it works just as well this way. We hope so.

NEVER HAD IT SO GOOD

In October 1959 Harold MacMillan's Conservative government was standing for re-election, and so the Minster of Transport was unavailable for the opening of the Chiswick flyover, that would, in 1965, become the eastern end of the M4. They couldn't get Stirling Moss or Donald Campbell, and so, as a last resort, they persuaded Jayne Mansfield to do the honours. She was at MGM's Boreham Wood studios filming 'Too hot to handle', and popped over to cut the ribbon on 11 am on Wednesday 30th September 1959.

Kew Gardens

We're only a few hundred metres from the Thames at the point where Kew inhabits the south bank. Hopefully one day the National Botanical Gardens of Wales at the other end of the M4 will blossom into an equal for this place, which has a charm that doesn't grow on trees.

HISTORY

In 1896 the speed limit on English roads was raised from 4 mph to 14 mph. Toad of Toad Hall was out of his box.

Soon number plates were introduced to identify individual vehicles for the first time. (This would solve the problem of witnesses saying: "I think there was a frog in plus fours and goggles at the wheel").

In 1904 you could buy a Standard 7 Jarrott for £150: "a self-powered, open-topped, horseless carriage with a leather bench seat and a dashboard." And there were 3,000 motorised taxis serving London.

Next year the speed limit was raised to 20 mph, the Automobile Association came into being and the Siddeley Motor Car Company claimed their vehicles could do 5,000 miles without breaking down.

By 1906 there were 700 motorised buses travers-ing the capital's streets.

Just before the First World War the first Morris car was built in a garage in Cowley in Oxfordshire; meanwhile Henry Ford switched on his constant-ly-moving assembly line and churned out a Model T in 3 hours, allowing him to produce a quarter of a million of them in that first year.

By 1920 there were 350,000 cars and lorries on British roads, and the motor industry was manufacturing 34,000 new vehicles each year.

You could buy a new Morgan runabout in Malvern for £95 in 1925, but go to jail for being found drunk at the wheel.

Driving tests were made compulsory In 1928, when the Morris Minor was launched, Hyde Park Corner was declared the world's busiest traffic junction and 14 people died each day in accidents on British roads.

In the early 1930s the Highway Code was published, and the first traffic policeman was deployed. Every motorist now had to have third party insurance and houses began to be built with garages alongside.

There were over 2.5 million vehicles on British roads in 1936, of which 400,000 were vans.

By 1955 there were 3.5 million cars on our roads, and plans were afoot to construct the first British motorways.

The Chiswick flyover, which became the eastern end of the M4, opened in 1959.

The Paris motor show of that year was dominated by British cars: BMC's Farina range, the Aston Martin DB4, the Sunbeam Alpine and Rapier models.

President de Gaulle was especially interested in the £589 Ford Anglia.

Improvements to the A4 continued with the Hammersmith flyover, and the widening of the Great West Road, and the creation of the Maidenhead by-pass, all operational by 1961.

Around the same time contracts were issued for the construction of the Severn Bridge, the Slough by-pass and the Chiswick elevated section above the Great West Road. This eastern-most length was constructed by Marples Ridgeway, Ernest Marples being a director and major sharehold-er, as well as Minister of Transport.

The Slough by-pass took two years to construct, the Chiswick viaduct three years and the Severn crossing five years.

Then, undoubtedly encouraged by the closure of a third of the railway network in 1963, all that needed to be done was to join those bits up.

The A46 south of Chipping Sodbury (Junction 18) was connected to the embryonic M5 at Almondsbury in 1966.

Great debate delayed plans to create a route from Junction 18 (Tormarton) to Slough. Charlesworth's History of British Motorways explains the complicated options that challenged consulting engineers Sir Alexander Gibb. It was not obvious whether to go north or south of Reading. And horse training interests around the Lambourne Downs brought heavy lobbying to bear on the alternatives.

In all over 1,000 miles of route were examined before settling on the final 80 mile track - generally gentlemanly battles and small beer compared to the blood letting that ensued upon the announcement of a Newbury by-pass.

The Tormarton to Slough carriageway was completed in 1971, and perhaps those respected arguments by wealthy landowners explain why this segment includes some of the most sightless sections of motorway in the country.

The M5 ran fully northward towards the Midlands in that same year, but it was another three years before it could cross the River Avon south of Bristol.

Charlesworth doesn't devote much attention to the only motorway in Wales, co-ordinated by the Director of Transport and Highways Group in Cardiff.

There had been aspirations to bridge the Severn estuary dating back to Thomas Telford's time. His motive had been to substantially reduce mail coach journey times to and from Milford Haven.

A Parliamentary Bill was proposed in the 1930s to create a crossing to take the traffic out of Chepstow, but this was defeated by lobbying from the Great Western Railway Company who didn't want competition for their tunnel or bridge (the latter, much further upstream, was damaged beyond repair in the 1960s).

After the Second World War there was a pressing need for effective by-passes around Newport, Port Talbot and Neath and a perception of the economic advantages of making the Valleys more accessible for future work as the coal and steel prospects declined. Glamorganshire County Surveyors vigorously advanced a variety of schemes, then in November 1967 the Welsh Office got a grip on the sundry elements and announced plans for the whole route, relatively little of which generated much in the way of objections or Public Inquiries, with the exception of the stretch north of Cardiff.

Port Talbot by-pass opened in 1966, and Newport by-pass in 1967. This included Britain's first motorway tunnel and thirty years after it opened, they wish they had made it three lanes wide rather than just two. Swansea by-pass opened in 1972.

Most of the rest came into effect in 1977, the bit round Cardiff opened in 1980 and the bit round Bridgend in 1981, and they widened what they could around Newport in the same year.

There's now talk of a second Newport by-pass running south of the city as a way of relieving the existing thoroughfare.

At 204 miles, the M4 is the second longest motorway of the big four (M1: 194; M5: 168; M6: 234).

Hard to put a defining date on the opening of the M4, because of the piecemeal fashion of its creation. Technically, the Chiswick-Langley section was the first proper stretch, and this was declared open by Minister of Transport Tom Fraser on Wednesday 24th March 1965, though bits of it had been in use since November 1964. To mark the occasion the Bishop of London said a prayer for the safety of the new highway.

We are drawn back to the earlier event. 11.00am on Wednesday 30th September 1959, when Jayne Mansfield was chauffeured down from Elstree "in a skin tight crimson dress" to "gaily snip a red ribbon with gold-plated scissors" (Daily Mail 1st October) opening the Chiswick flyover, which patently is the very first bit of the M4. Of course eight years later the glamorous American movie star died in a car accident in Louisiana, so she's probably not a good icon for travellers. But we can't help feeling this was the most memorable moment in M4 history. Day One, in fact.

There are now over 30 million vehicles on British roads. 2.5 million cars are bought in Britain each year, and on average we commute 8.5 miles to work, which takes 45 minutes. We are the most committed commuters in Europe, and most of us do it on our own - 13 million of us a day.

Only one in seven of us reaches work by public transport. Britain's biggest concentration of long distance commuting is via the M4, a considerable proportion of people travelling more than 35 miles each way every day – yes, from Reading to London and back.

On World Environment Day 2005, Alastair Darling announced intentions to explore pricing policy for vehicle use.

A typical day sees 93,000 vehicles using some part of the M4. Some days the figure reaches 150,000.

Regulars users have our sympathy. We hope this Guide makes those journeys better.

Finally, a sight that doesn't even lie on the M4, but for many represents its gateway. The Ark at Hammersmith. Ralph Erskine's iconic structure (currently unoccupied) sits to the south of the A4, just east of the flyover. For those leaving London via the M4, it says you're on your way. For those reaching the city, it says you've arrived. Erskine died on 16th March 2005, aged 91. The Guardian's obituary described him as a visionary architect with social and environmental commitment.

WELSH NAMES

Beth yw ystyr y gair yna?

That's Welsh for: What does that mean?

We don't think we were alone in driving along the M4 in Wales and thinking Abertawe was a different place from Swansea.

For design reasons we have only used the English names in our entries and so here we give you what appears in Welsh above or below the English names, west to east.

Carmarthenshire
Sir Gaerfyrddin
Pronounced: s-ee-r G-ie-r-vUrr-th-in

Ammanford
Rhydaman
Pronounced: reed-A-man
Meaning: Ford of the River Amman

Pont Abraham Services
Gwasanaethau Pont Abraham
Pronounced: gwas-an-IE-th-ie pont Ah-bra-ham
Meaning: Abraham's Bridge

National Botanical Garden
Gardd Fotaneg Genedlaethol
Pronounced: gar-th vo-tAn-eg gen-ed-LIE-th-ol

Carmarthen
Caerfyrddin
Pronounced: k-ie-r-vUrr-th-in
Meaning: Fort at Maridunum (name of Roman settlement at the site)

St Clears
Sancler
Pronounced: san-kLAIr

City and County of Swansea
Dinas a Sir Abertawe
Pronounced: dEE-nas ah S-EE-r ah-bair-TAh-weh

Pembrey Country Park
Parc Gwledig Penbre
Pronounced: park goo-LED-ig pen-brEh
Meaning: Top of the burrows (reference to the extensive sand dunes of the area)

Swansea Enterprise Park
Parc Anturiaeth Abertawe
Pronounced: park an-tEEr-ee-ei-th a-bair-tA-weh

Swansea
Abertawe
Pronounced: a-bair-tA-weh
Meaning: Mouth of the River Tawe (pronounced tAH-weh)

West
Gorllewin
Pronounced: gor-LL-E-win

Central
Canol
Pronounced: kAn-ol

East
Dwyrain
Pronounced: doo-EE-rine

South
De
Pronounced: dEh

Briton Ferry
Llansawel
Pronounced: Llan-sAh-wel
Meaning: Saul's Church

Neath
Castell-Nedd
Pronounced: kAst-eLL nEh-th
Meaning: Castle on the Nedd river (this fort was named "Nidum" by the Romans, after the river's Celtic name)

Vale of Neath
Cwm Nedd
Pronoounced: koom nEh-th

Aberavon
Aberafan
Pronounced: a-bair-A-van
Meaning: Mouth of the river Afan

Margam Crematorium
Amlosgfa Margam
Pronounced: am-LOsk-va mAr-gam

Cardiff Airport
Maes Awyr Caerdydd
Pronounced: mice Ah-wee-r k-ie-r-dEE-th

Pyle
Pil
Pronounced: P-ee-l
Meaning: Tidal creek

County Borough of Bridgend
Bwrdeisdref Sirol Pen-y-bont
Pronounced: boord-ICE-drehv sEE-rol pen-uh-bOnt

Bridgend
Pen-y-bont
Pronounced: pen-uh-bOnt
Meaning: End of the Bridge

Rhondda Heritage Park
Parc Treftadaeth Cwm Rhondda
Pronounced: park trehv-tAH-die-th koom rOn-tha

Museum of Welsh Life
Amgueddfa Werin Cymru
Pronounced: am-g-ee-Eth-va wEH-rin kUm-ree

Barry Island
Ynys y Barri
Pronounced: Unn-iss uh bA-ree

Cardiff Bay
Bae Caerdydd
Pronounced: by k-ie-r-dEE-th

Caerphilly
Caerffili
Pronounced: k-ie-r-fEE-lee

Cardiff
Caerdydd
Pronounced: k-ie-r-dEE-th
Meaning: Fort on the River Taff

Cardiff Gate
Porth Caerdydd
Pronounced: po-r-th k-ie-r-dEE-th

City and County of Cardiff
Dinas a Sir Caerdydd
Pronounced: dEE-nas ah sEE-r k-ie-r-dEE-th

Capital of Wales
Prifddinas Cymru
Pronounced: preev-thEEn-as kUm-ree

Festival Park
Parc Yr Wyl
Pronounced: park uh-r OO-ee-l

Forest Drive
Rhodfa'r Coed
Pronounced: rOd-va-r k-oy-d

Tredegar House
Ty Tredegar
Pronounced: tee tred-Eh-ga-r

Big Pit
Pwll Mawr
Pronounced: poo-ll mA-oo-r

Roman Fortress/remains
Caer Rhufeinig
Pronounced: k-ei-r reev-INE-ig

Newport Docks
Dociau Casnewydd
Pronounced: dOk-ee-ie kas-nE-with

Newport
Casnewydd
Pronounced: kas-nE-with
Meaning: New Castle (Cas is a shortened form of "Castell")

Magor Services
Gwasanaethau Magor
Pronounced: gwas-an-IE-th-ie mA-gor
Meaning: Bulwarks, fortifications

Chepstow
Cas gwent
Pronounced: kas-gwEnt
Meaning: Castle of Gwent

Monmouth
Trefynwy
Pronounced: treh-VUN-wee
Meaning: Town on the River Mynwy (Monnow)

Monmouthshire
Sir Fynwy
Pronounced: s-ee-r VUN-wee

Welcome to Wales
Croeso i Gymru
Pronounced: krOY-so ee gUm-ree

Key to imitated pronunciation:
Capital letters indicate stressed syllable – if you emphasize this part of the word you'll get much closer to the correct balance of the Welsh pronunciation.

1) There's no easy equivalent in English to help you make the LL... sound! You'll need to keep the tip of your tongue in contact with the ridge of the gums of your upper front teeth and gently expel your breath along both sides of the tongue. Try it with Llan first!

2) "th" – as in English "the", or "then" (this is the mysterious "dd" sound!)

3) "th" – as in English "thin" or "think"

4) "ie" – as in "pie" or "tie"

5) Try to roll any "r"s that are given in the imitated pronunciation – as you would when pronouncing the "r" in "thrill"

6) "uh" as the "a" sound in "I bought a book"

Pronounce the rest of the imitated pronunciation equivalents as you would in English and you'll be very close to the correct sounds for the Welsh word or expression. Take your time, syllable by syllable (many find it easier starting with the last syllable first!), and then speed it up – and you'll soon be sounding like a siaradwr brodorol or native speaker!

Ian Davies
Museum of Welsh Life.

THE M48

Chepstow

An important port and crossing point at the mouth of the Wye for centuries, captured with excellent artefacts in the museum housed opposite the impressive castle. The magnificent headquarters of the Chepstow Bank dominated the town square from 1850 to 1969, when it was knocked down to be replaced by a nondescript branch of Barclays, that remains in prime position and takes some shine off millions of pounds worth of worthwhile town centre regeneration.

BEACHLEY BARRACKS

St George's Chapel sits within the temporary home of 500 members of the 1st Battalion of the Green Howards, the oldest unamalgamated regiment in the British Army. They hail from north Yorkshire and may become the 2nd Battalion of the Yorkshire Regiment soon. In the spring of 2005 they had just returned from a successful term of duty in Afghanistan.

OLD FERRY HOTEL (E.O.)

Good food in here that can be enjoyed while gazing across the estuary.

Superbly documented on wall panels by the landlord are details of the ferry service that ran between here and Aust from the 1920s until – yes, you've guessed it – the first M4 motorway bridge opened.

BROADWELL FARM (E.O.)

Behind this home to many horses there was once the village of Runston, but all that remains are fragments of the church. The settlement declined and then disappeared in the 1700s, due to hardship and ill health.

WYELANDS (E.O.)

This coach house was first built in 1700. It was briefly the Wyelands estate's dedicated dance hall in WW2, and later became derelict. Now it's a £750,000 conversion.

CONTINUES WEST ON PAGE 37.

ST PIERRE'S

Secreted away from the riff-raff were a series of private estates round here. Biggest was that of the St Pierre's, a French family (surprise, surprise) who eventually saw fit to change their name to Lewis (with the aim of fitting in better, perhaps). They also occupied some swanky outbuildings, not least Moynes Court, now split into private homes, visible to us passing riff-raff through the trees. These days St Pierre's is a hotel and golf club.

NEWPORT–GLOUCESTER

Arriva services between Cardiff and Gloucester run along the western edge of the Severn estuary about once an hour during a typical weekday. Nice ride, good views.

TESCO (W.O.)

1,800 articulated lorry loads leave this south west chilled and frozen distribution centre each week, mostly containing cages of products for a single store. 178 vehicles operate out of the 57 bays - which means nationally Tesco must have one of the largest fleet of liveried vehicles, not far behind Royal Mail in numbers. Seeing them here in such density was like spotting the German army amassing on the Polish border.

ASDA

The British arm of Wal-Mart, with a mere 279 UK stores, compared with Morrisons, checking in at 435 (including the Safeways being re-branded), Sainsbury's @ 727, Tesco @ 1,200 and the Co-op's 1,700.

RIVER WYE

There was considerable ship-building around the mouth of the river, both for sea-going vessels and for river-plying trows. Frequently carrying timber or grain, trows would sometime drift into the piers of Chepstow bridge, be holed, and then "settle down".

ARMY APPRENTICE COLLEGE (W.O.)

This opened on the Beachley peninsula in 1933 and at its height had an intake of 500 16-year olds a year, learning every type of trade before being assigned to a regiment. Padre Joe Rooney told us they turned out enough people with sufficient skills to build a town. Now it's just a temporary home for army units, who can use this 30 metre armament range.

OLDBURY NUCLEAR POWER STATION

Twin reactors can supply enough electricity to serve Bristol. Operational since 1967 and due to be decommissioned in 2008. Visitor Centre open weekdays from 10.30 – 3.30 in the summer months, but all station tours are suspended.

SEVERN VIEW SERVICES

Initially a tourist destination in its own right attracting people from all over Europe to admire the feat of bridging the Severn so successfully, this is now a modest place. An inscribed stone outside the main building commemorates PC Stephen Jones who was killed here whilst apprehending criminals on 17th May 1999.

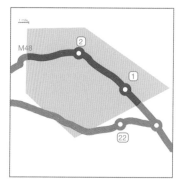

FERRY SERVICES

These have been in operation across the estuary since Roman times. The Old Passage between Beachley and Aust was free for mediaeval monks, their servants and cattle. A New Passage service further south commenced in 1752. The boat was moored on the Welsh side at Black Rock near Portskewett. Passengers on the east wishing to use it had to set fire to a pile of straw to attract the attention of the skipper.

MOTION MEDIA TECHNOLOGY CENTRE

This building once housed the popular restaurant for the Severn View motorway service area. Now it's home to a couple of video phone businesses.

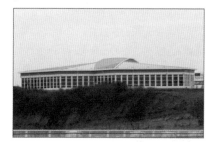

COTE LODGE (W.O.)

This dates from 1856, when Aust still traded on boat crossings of the estuary. There's a pair of old Bowser petrol pumps on a stone plinth in the village itself, outside what was the post office.

M48 CONTINUES EAST ON PAGE 40

TOLLS - SEE PAGE 37

J1

NATIONAL GRID PYLON

They don't come much bigger than this. It's 471 metres high and carries 275,000 volts.

FIRST SEVERN BRIDGE

Work commenced in 1961. The main span is 1,000 metres and the towers supporting the cables are 130 metres high. The piers carrying the towers each consist of 30,000 cubic metres of concrete, the anchorages for the cable ends 100,000 cubic metres. Each steel tower weighs 1,300 tons and carries a vertical dead load of 13,200 tons. Each cable is half a metre wide and made up of 8,322 separate wires manufactured in Middlesbrough. The bridge was opened by the Queen on 8th September 1966 and has so far carried 300 million vehicles. Picture: Page 39.

CHAPELRY OF ST JOHN, AUST

When we called, monumental mason Mr Cottle was about to bring in a two hundredweight granite inscribed headstone for a one year old grave. They cost about £400 plus VAT, plus church fees (£150) and take a week to prepare. In his fifty year career he's inscribed a few wrong letters and numerals, mostly because distressed relatives have given him incorrect information, but not every time.

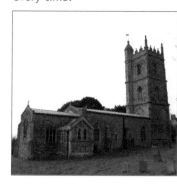

SECOND SEVERN CROSSING

See page 38.

THE M32 LINKS TO THE M4 ON OUR PAGES 42 AND 43.

DOWER HOUSE

We really only included the M32 to embrace this place, which dates back to 1750, became the noble Beauforts' Bristol address from 1770, was sold off to mental health pioneer Harold Burden as a hospital in 1901, and is now becoming swanky apartments with unrivalled views of the M32.

Filton

It's where Concorde came from and went to – landing for the final time on 26th November 2003. Always a pioneering centre of British aircraft production, the place took a hammering during WW2 (along with many other parts of Bristol), the German Luftwaffe sometimes deploying over 100 bombers a night.

OBELISK STUMP

We translated the plate in Latin on the side to find out it was done up last year as a tribute to "Elizabetha Somerset Caroll Ducis Beaufort".

Horfield

In the library they have a copy of 'An Account of Horfield from Early Times to 1900' by Rev. Fanshawe Bingham. Amongst many delights, it documents how a predecessor sustained himself during Sunday morning services by munching sugar lumps soaked in cognac.

PURDOWN RADIO STATION

This was built in 1961 and is over 60 metres high. BT explained to us that it "plays an important part in network telecommunications", which probably means those big microwave dishes are bouncing TV pictures, amongst other things, in and out of both the BBC and ITV West in Bristol.

FAIRFIELD SCHOOL

No, not smart new apartments but a huge, new 1,200 pupil place, taking over the site from St Thomas More RC School.

TESCO

One of the top three largest retailers in the world, thus statistically bringing joy and satisfaction to the lives of millions. Extra at Eastville, with 33 check-outs, has recently gone 24 hours.

IKEA

The contents of flat-packs that have gone seriously wrong are put on to cages in the car park. You can help yourself to this chipboard or timber, from which it shouldn't be impossible to construct a free shelving unit.

FILTON–TEMPLE MEADS

Services from Wales and the north of England approach the Bristol terminus along here. A parallel track carries the local commuter loop, that swings over to Avonmouth and Shirehampton.

BRISTOL DECORATIVE SURFACES

They make Formica seem sexy, and do other interior finishes, including something called Wetwall panelling: "a stylish alternative to tiles, and Axiom work surfaces where "style becomes eclectic."

BL FLOORING

This is a family firm who supply adhesives to the laminated flooring trade. Manning the fort on a Saturday morning, Jodie Burt told us of the sticky situation when their van did an emergency stop, tipping out the contents of the tubs.

ST WERBURGH'S COMMUNITY CENTRE

A fantastic array of honourable grass roots organisations operate from this old school where you can attend courses on a vast spectrum of alternative interests, from Narcotics Anonymous to Bollywood Dancing.

J2

THE M32

This is the only pair of pages in this book showing the carriageway running from top to bottom, as it mostly does in our previous titles. We have not included designations for orange boxes or angles of view. Doubtless most users know what they can see a lot better than we do.

Fishponds

Dedicated slave trade abolitionist Hannah More was born here in 1745. She campaigned vigorously both in Bristol and London and supported William Wilberforce with Parliamentary lobbying in the 1770s.

LINDEN HOUSE

Smart apartments on the site of another old Bristol hospital - Purdown.

MANOR PARK HOSPITAL

Originally a military prison, it became a workhouse in the 19th century, then a hospital after WW1. It's now also the University of the West of England's Faculty of Health and Social Care.

HOLY TRINITY CHURCH, STAPLETON

Indicates the location of Colston's School, where 900 pupils gain a "superior independent education". Perhaps some of the pupils end up across the carriageway (behind the Bristol Business Park) at the University of the West of England's Faculty for the Built Environment doing BA (Hons) Planning with Transport.

e-petitions

If there are things about Bristol you don't like, you can start a petition by visiting www.bristol-city.gov.uk/epetitions. An initiative of the Council's corporate consultation. Go on, try one and start a trend.

MERCHANTS ARMS

Trading as the Hungry Horse. When we looked in on a Saturday afternoon, it was catering for a lot of people who looked like a diet would be better for them. Nice range of nautical memorabilia on show.

NEW TESTAMENT CHURCH OF GOD, EASTVILLE

A warm Pentecostal welcome to all from Revd R.B. Brown, Minister.

SHAH JALAL JAME MOSQUE

The Bandladesh community initiated and manage the first purpose-built mosque in the South West, designed by a Birmingham Muslim architect, and serving 10,000 Muslims, who often combine visits with shopping on Stapleton Road.

PHARMACY PLUS

A family firm delivering customised packages of drugs to nursing homes and medical centres.

OLD FOX INN

A free house with real ale. Round the back a sign says "Kerb crawlers will be arrested."

GREEK ORTHODOX CHURCH

Father George explained to us how the Greek Cypriot community acquired this semi-derelict Anglical church in the 1960s and steadily improved the property and facilities, which now attracts up to 1,000 worshippers at Easter. No-one wanted to lop the top off the steeple, but it was in a dangerous condition and would have cost far too much to re-build in its original form.

BRISTOL FRUIT SALES

They've got about a fifth of the Bristol fruit and veg business, but a bigger public profile thanks to their 8 distinctive vehicles trafficking bananas from their ripening sheds to supermarkets and wholesale outlets around the south west. Each of their chilled artics carries 26 pallets, each holding 48 boxes, each containing about 100 bananas.

JUNCTION 3

The M32 ends at Junction 3. Biggest building directly ahead is Tollgate House, once occupied by the Department of the Environment, but now destined for demolition.

INDEX

BIBLIOGRAPHY

Alfred Russel Wallace — George Eaton

And so make a city here — G.E. Bate

Another 22 organisations — S.T.E.A.M.

Berkshire Book — Berkshire W.I.

Berkshire Churches — Mark Chatfield

Berkshire — Arthur Mee

Book of the Thames — Mr and Mrs S.C. Hall

Bradfield College — Arthur F. Leach

British Canals — Charles Hadfield

Caerleon Endowed Schools — T.M. Morgan

Chepstow Scrapbook — Ivor Waters

Chilterns to Black Country — W.G. Hoskins

Chiswick Past and Present — Gillian Clegg

Contour Roadbook — Harry R.G. Inglis

The Cruel Inheritance — Roger Williams & David Jones

Discovering the Bath Road — Margaret Baker

Down the Line to Bristol — Muriel V. Searle

The Fed — Hywel Francis & David Smith

Gorseinon & District — Keith E. Morgan

Great Road to Bath — Daphne Phillips

Gwent — Bobby Freeman

History of Port Talbot — Sally Roberts Jones

History of British Motorways — George Charlesworth

History of Swindon — Mike Childs

Horfield Miscellanea — Fanshawe Bingham

How we can save the planet — Mayer Hillman

Hungerford — Walter Money

Illustrated Guide to GWR — George Measom

The Kennet — Wilson Stephens

London Orbital — Iain Sinclair

M25 — Roy Phippen

The Merthyr Rising — Gwyn A. Williams

Middlesex — Norman G. Brett-James

Midland & South Western — David Bartholomew

Motorists Companion — Christopher Trent

Murray's Berkshire — John Betjeman & John Piper

Not on the Label — Felicity Lawrence

Off the Motorway — Paul and Shirley Smith

Only Just — Gordon Rollinson

Powerhouse of Industry — Association for Industrial Archaeology

Profile of a Welsh Town — J. Ivor Hanson

Racehorse Trainers — David Boyd

Railway Atlas — Alan Jowett

Railways of Wales — Gwyn Briwant Jones & Denis Dunstone

Reading Football Club — Alan Sedunary

Remembrance of a Riot — John Edwards

Reminiscences of Briton Ferry — E. Humphries

Risca — Alan Victor Jones

Royal Ascot — George Cawthorne & Richard Herod

Severn Railway Tunnel — Roger Cowles

Severn Tunnel — Thomas A Walker

Shopped — Joanna Blythman

State of Gloucestershire — Sir Robert Atkyns

Story of Newbury — Tony Higgott

Swindon Railway Village — Karen E Whatley

Taff Vale Railway — D.S. Barrie

Theale Social Survey — J. Goaman & R.S. Every

Transport in Britain — Philip Bagwell & Peter Lyth

Welsh Heretic — T. Islwyn Nicholas

Welsh Steel — Robert Protheroe-Jones

Wiltshire Machine Breakers — Jill Chambers

Wiltshire Villages — Margaret Wilson

Wokingham and District — W.J. Gotelee

The World we're in — Will Hutton

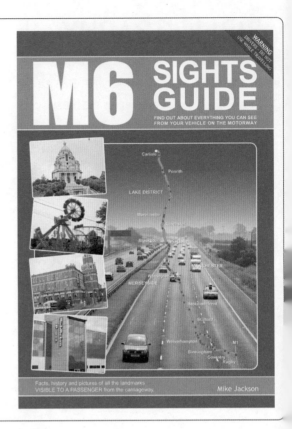